PLATO'S WISDOM HANDBOOK

EQUIP YOURSELF WITH TIMELESS INSIGHTS THAT
WILL HELP GUIDE YOU IN THESE MODERN TIMES

WISDOM UNIVERSITY

CONTENTS

Exclusive Offer ... 1
What Reader's Are Saying About Wisdom University ... 9
Introduction: Experience Growth Mindset ... 13

1. Navigating Plato ... 18
   How To Read Plato Your Own Way

2. Youth, War, And Socratic Influence ... 26
   What Drives The Path To Becoming A Philosopher

3. The Trial ... 44
   What Wonderment And A Wise Mentor Can Do For Our Pursuit Of Truth

4. Distant Ideals No More ... 63
   What Is Plato's Theory Of Forms And How Do They Shape Our Perceptions

5. Parmenides Versus Plato ... 83
   How To Probe The Nature Of Reality, Change, And The Limits Of Human Understanding

6. Plato's Famous Cave Allegory ... 100
   How To Step Into The Light And Walk Toward The Truth In Your Everyday Life

7. Bask In The Philosopher King's Glory ... 112
   What Does It Take To Become A Wise Successful Leader

8. An Ethical Inquiry ... 129
   How Cardinal Values Keep The Soul Healthy

9. The Perfect Society ... 138
   What A Philosopher's Utopia Teaches Us About Good Government In These Changing Times

10. Echoes Of Plato ... 160
    How Plato's Insights Shape Modern Disciplines And Influence The Way We Think Today

Conclusion: The Philosopher's Gift	173
Your Last Chance For Our Limited Deal	177
The People Behind Wisdom University	179
References	183
Disclaimer	203

Exclusive Offer

4 Bonuses + Free Access To ALL Our Upcoming Books!

Free Bonus #1
Our Bestseller
How To Train Your Thinking
Total Value: $9.99

If you're ready to take maximum control of your finances and career, then keep reading...

Here's just a fraction of what you'll discover inside:
- Why hard work has almost nothing to do with making money, and what the real secret to wealth is
- Why feeling like a failure is a great place to start your success story
- The way to gain world-beating levels of focus, even if you normally struggle to concentrate

"This book provides a wealth of information on how to improve your thinking and your life. It is difficult to summarize the information provided. When I tried, I found I was just listing the information provided on the contents page. To obtain the value provided in the book, you must not only read and understand the provided information, you must apply it to your life."

NealWC - Reviewed in the United States on July 16, 2023

"This is an inspirational read, a bit too brainy for me as I enjoy more fluid & inspirational reads. However, the author lays out the power of thought in a systematic way!"

Esther Dan - Reviewed in the United States on July 13, 2023

"This book offers clear and concise methods on how to think. I like that it provides helpful methods and examples about the task of thinking. An insightful read for sharpening your mind."

Demetrius - Reviewed in the United States on July 16, 2023

"Exactly as the title says, actionable steps to guide your thinking! Clear and concise."

Deirdre Hagar Virgillo - Reviewed in the United States on July 18, 2023

"This is a book that you will reference for many years to come. Very helpful and a brain changer in you everyday life, both personally and professionally. Enjoy!"

Skelly - Reviewed in the United States on July 6, 2023

Free Bonus #2
Our Bestseller
The Art Of Game Theory
Total Value: $9.99

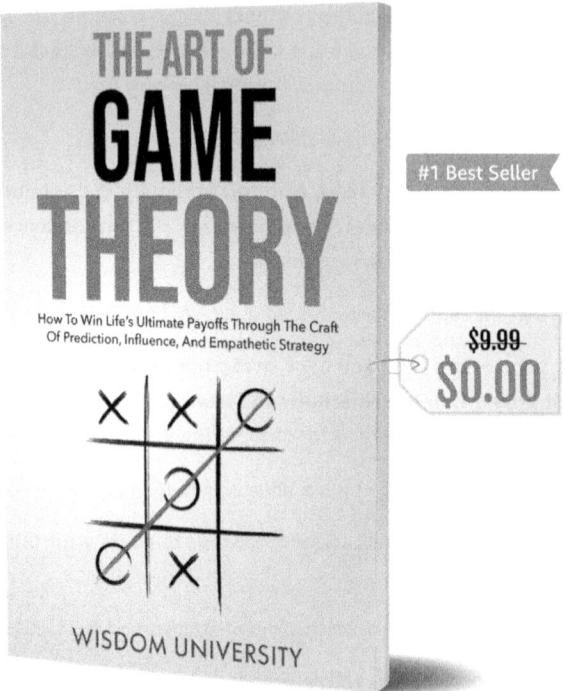

If Life is a game, what are the rules? And more importantly... Where are they written?

Here's just a fraction of what you'll discover inside:
- When does it pay to be a selfish player... and why you may need to go inside a prisoner's mind to find out
- How to recognize which game you're playing and turn the tables on your opponent... even if they appear to have the upper hand
- Why some games aren't worth playing and what you should do instead

"Thanks Wisdom University! This book offers simple strategies one can use to achieve things in your personal life. Anyone of average intelligence can read, understand and be in a position to enact the suggestions contained within."

David L. Jones - Reviewed in the United States on November 12, 2023

"Haven't finished it yet, but what I've gone through so far is just incredible! Another great job from this publisher!"

W. S. Jones - Reviewed in the United States on October 12, 2023

"A great book to help you through difficult and complex problems. It gets you to think differently about what you are dealing with. Highly recommend to both new and experienced problem solvers. You with think differently after reading this book."

Thom - Reviewed in the United States on October 18, 2023

"I like this book and how it simplifies complex ideas into something to use in everyday life. I am applying the concept and gaining a lot of clarity and insight."

Ola - Reviewed in the United States on October 18, 2023

"The book is an excellent introduction to game theory. The writing is clear, and the analysis is first-rate. Concrete, real-world examples of theory are presented, and both the ways in which game theory effectively models what actually happens in life is cogently evaluated. I also appreciate the attention paid to the ethical dimensions of applying game theory in many situations."

Amazon Customer - Reviewed in the United States on October 8, 2023

Free Bonus #3
Thinking Cheat Sheet
Break Your Thinking Patterns
Total Value: $4.99

Free Bonus #4
Thinking Sheet
Flex Your Wisdom Muscle
Total Value: $4.99

A glimpse into what you'll discover inside:
- How to expose the sneaky flaws in your thinking and what it takes to fix them (the included solutions are dead-simple)
- Dozens of foolproof strategies to make sound and regret-free decisions leading you to a life of certainty and fulfillment
- How to elevate your rationality to extraordinary levels (this will put you on a level with Bill Gates, Elon Musk and Warren Buffett)
- Hidden gems of wisdom to guide your thoughts and actions (gathered from the smartest minds of all time)

Bonus #5

Get ALL our upcoming books for FREE
(Yes, you've read that right)
Total Value: $199.80*

You'll get exclusive access to our books before they hit the online shelves and enjoy them for free.

Here's everything you get:

- ✓ How To Train Your Thinking eBook — ($9.99 Value)
- ✓ The Art Of Game Theory eBook — ($9.99 Value)
- ✓ Break Your Thinking Patterns Sheet — ($4.99 Value)
- ✓ Flex Your Wisdom Muscle Sheet — ($4.99 Value)
- ✓ All our upcoming eBooks — ($199.80* Value)

Total Value: $229.76

Take me to wisdom-university.net for my free bonuses!

(Or simply scan the code with your camera)

Scan Me

*If you download 20 of our books for free, this would equal a value of 199.80$

WHAT READER'S ARE SAYING ABOUT WISDOM UNIVERSITY

"I have been reading books from Wisdom University for a while now and have been impressed with the CONDENSED AND VALUABLE INFORMATION they contain. Reading these books allows me to LEARN INFORMATION QUICKLY AND EASILY, so I can put the knowledge to practice right away to improve myself and my life. I recommend it for busy people who don't have a LOT of time to read, but want to learn: Wisdom University gives you the opportunity to easily and quickly learn a lot of useful, practical information, which helps you have a better, more productive, successful, and happier life. It takes the information and wisdom of many books and distills and organizes the most useful and helpful information down into a smaller book, so you spend more time applying helpful information, rather than reading volumes of repetition and un-needed filler text.

—*Dawn Campo, Degree in Human psychology and Business, Office administrator from Utah*

"Wisdom University produces great books. Concise information and valuable knowledge to help us in this long journey that is self-improvement."

—*Bruno Estevanato, MBA, Banker in Brazil*

retired Computer Programmer

"Wisdom University embodies an innovative and progressive educational approach, expertly merging deep academic insights with contemporary learning techniques. Their books are not only insightful and captivating but also stand out for their emphasis on practical application, making them a valuable resource for both academic learning and real-world personal development."

—*Bryan Kornele, 55 years old, Software Engineer from the United States*

"WU's emails discuss interesting topics. They have good offers. I can recommend the books to my My friends and relatives."

—Wilbur Dudley, Louisiana (USA), 77, BS in Business Administration and DBA, retired

"I have most of the ebooks & audiobooks that Wisdom University has created. I prefer audiobooks as found on

Audible. The people comprising Wisdom University do an excellent job of providing quality personal development materials. They offer value for everyone interested in self-improvement."

—*Neal Cheney, double major in Computer-Science & Mathematics, retired 25yrs USN (Nuclear Submarines) and retired Computer Programmer*

"Wisdom University teaches factual Management Techniques. I would recommend their books to any managers."

—*Brett Gaskin, MSc in Physics, Senior Quality Manager in the high-tech industry*

"I wanted to read some books about thinking and learning which have some depth. I can say "Wisdom University" is one of the most valuable and genuine brands I have ever seen. Their books are top-notch at kindle. I have read their books on learning, thinking, etc. & they are excellent. I would especially recommend their latest book "Think Like Da Vinci" to those who want to have brilliant & clear thinking."

—*Sahil Zen, 20 years old from India, BSc student of Physics*

"I associate Wisdom University with critical thinking and knowledge improvement. It is helpful for critical thinkers and all those who are interested in improving their knowledge."

—Elliot Wilson, MBA and Doctor of Business Administration (DBA), Chief Growth Officer

INTRODUCTION: EXPERIENCE GROWTH MINDSET

HOW PLATO'S DIALOGUES HELP US EXPAND OUR CRITICAL THINKING

"We can easily forgive a child who is afraid of the dark," Plato is thought to have said. "The real tragedy of life is when men are afraid of the light." [1]

Going into the light means reckoning with knowledge and truth using critical thinking to better assess everything you experience. If you're lucky, you may grow just as wise as Socrates, Plato's beloved teacher, and be able to say you actually know very little at all.

Perhaps you're wondering what a 2,500-year-old philosopher can possibly have to say about your life. Keep asking questions. Questioning is good. It goes to the heart of what Plato and Socrates, too, were all about. And asking questions instead of just assuming may yield answers that surprise you.

Learning about Plato benefits everyone, and this book could especially help if you:

- Have trouble connecting in your relationships
- Second-guess the direction of your life and choices
- Want personal and professional mentorship
- Need an attaboy about where you are in your life

Distance in relationships can lead to withdrawal and depression, which in turn can stunt mental growth and start a vicious self-defeating cycle. The self-defeating cycle intensifies when second-guessing fosters the gaslight effect, except you're doing it to yourself instead of having it done to you. Lack of guidance creates the feeling of being lost or adrift, further widening the gap in relationships, and needing feedback on your standing in life on a regular basis undercuts self-reliance. These are issues that can have a tenacious effect on your mental health if not solved.

While Plato isn't a miracle cure-all, his work inspires many to boost their critical thinking skills in hopes of leading a happier, more enlightened life. Reading on, you will start on a knowledge-acquisition journey and get your questions answered… only to be replaced with more!

You will learn not only about Plato but yourself, too, discovering through reason the best path to set yourself on. In addition, you will attain the confidence to honor your preferences and needs, making and meeting the right goals for yourself.

Other learning points include 1) connecting with other people through dialogue, improving your relationships; 2) converting the confidence you gain into certainty regarding choices; 3) basking in the wisdom of Plato's example while discerning which of his ideas are most valuable to you; and 4) using progress made here to self-soothe about the rightness of additional strides you are making.

If you're not quite ready to dive in yet, consider your concerns and whether they can be addressed. For example:

"I don't have time to start a new book." If you're short on time, keep in mind that the Action Steps at the end of every chapter are quick and easy to incorporate. If you really need to, you can even start on an activity and then finish it the next day.

"It costs too much money." While money troubles are valid, the alternative in this case is missing out on a wealth of knowledge that can ease troubles that arise from uncertainty, distance from others, and lack of mentorship or feedback.

"Will this actually work?" As long as you develop a growth mindset over a fixed mindset, and are willing to learn, then yes. A 2018 study in which a two-and-a-half-hour computer-based "growth mindset intervention" (a program teaching growth mindset) was given to sixth, seventh, and eighth-grade students in Connecticut found that it positively impacted academic motivation. [2] The self-improvement promised here occurs in a motivated state, so keep reading with hunger.

"It's not the right time." Feeling some trepidation is only natural, for the techniques presented in this book will significantly change your life if wisely adapted. But if the issues you deal with daily are keeping you from growth, think about whether you really want to stay in this stagnant mindset.

"I don't need this." No, you don't, not in the same way you need food, water, and shelter. Philosophy is often misunderstood. It is thought of as an extraneous discipline, when in fact, much of it remains relevant and adaptable to your needs. You won't want to miss out when you realize what you'll miss: a guiding hand from Plato, a better understanding of self and others, greater certainty in making choices, and the satisfaction that accompanies self-improvement.

Plato directed us not to be afraid of the light. By stepping into the sun, you gain a sharper intellect that unlocks more of the right questions and possible answers to them, and you'll unlock one of the most sophisticated methods to reasoning in Western philosophy.

Who is making these promises, you may wonder? I am a seasoned storyteller who has published a literature paper interpreting "Antigone" and the "Apology" and presented a philosophy paper comparing Aristotle's environmental ethics to those in modern practice. Years of formal and self-study have honed my expertise in ancient Greek philosophy, nurturing a passion that has gripped me over the past ten years. I have a Bachelor's degree in creative writing and philosophy and wrote this book out of excitement to share my specialized knowledge in dual disciplines.

This book explores Plato's most eminent concepts, serves as a roadmap for more advanced critical thinking, and provides inspiration for self-starting with themed activities. It is *not* an exhaustive account of Plato's dialogues, an effortless path to genius, or Plato himself (there's room to disagree).

The book is designed to guide rather than lecture, relying on the Socratic Method to elicit self-discovery from students without laying the answer out for them. In Chapter 1, you will assess two possible reading orders of Plato's work and decide which one best suits your needs. Get ready to start sharpening your teeth on his most respected ideas. And, of course, have fun!

Zoe Grabow

1

NAVIGATING PLATO

HOW TO READ PLATO YOUR OWN WAY

Plato has given us so much material—36 dialogues—that it can be difficult to pick where to start.[1] We have a basic chronology for him (early, middle, late) but because he lived so long ago, even this is disputed. The other conventional order to read Plato is thematic, sorted by content rather than probable date.

There are pros and cons to each approach, and no right or wrong answer. Individual readers should pick one of these orders or come up with one of their own, according to how they best learn. The abundance of dialogues makes relative distance and closeness between works quite substantial, meaning that each order yields a distinct philosophical journey. The significance of drawing on themes vs. dates, or drawing on the differing historical contexts of dates vs. themes, changes how you experience the dialogues and the connections you make between them. Thus, order is quite important, but it doesn't erase the "choose-your-own-adventure" element that personalizes Plato to your needs.

Plato wrote in the dialogue format, an interesting technique that amps up engagement with the text. (You might even find yourself speaking aloud to the characters!) And written dialogue and spoken dialogue are more closely related than you might think. According to a 2023 study, word reading and listening comprehension in children are "moderately related," which shows the interconnectedness of the written and spoken word [2] and might explain why we feel we are experiencing Plato and his characters to an extent as we read his account. (It is perhaps noteworthy that his dialogues are formatted like plays, the genre being fundamentally interactive, with audience and actors sharing the same space.)

The study tested various reading and listening comprehension measures in 372 first-grade students, [3] and researchers watched for a connection through the direct and indirect effects model of reading, or DIER. DIER chalks reading comprehension up to "word reading, listening comprehension, text reading fluency, [and] background knowledge" among other factors and posits hierarchical, dynamic, and interactive relationships between components. [4]

Channeling this, the researchers assessed students using scales and tasks related to attentional control, working memory, phonological awareness, word reading, listening comprehension, reading comprehension, etc. For 30-40 minutes, students were given tasks to complete in the above component categories. [5]

Review of the students' performance of tasks found that "approximately 95% of variance in reading comprehension was explained by word reading and listening comprehension." [6] It added that the relationship weakened, but was still moderate, when components of working memory and attentional control were considered. In other words, reading skill and understanding of speech were the strongest correlates of solid reading comprehension, but adding in memory and attentiveness factors decreased the connection from a high correlation to a moderate one.

Encouragingly, a 2022 study found another written-spoken connection in a print-speech neural network, with adult convergence more sophisticated than a child's. Researchers ran fMRIs on 41 adults and 21 children who were given "print and speech word sound matching tasks," discovering that adults showed convergence in a greater concentration of areas in the brain, including "the left ventral and posterior regions, such as the inferior parietal area, middle temporal cortex and occipital regions." [7]

These regions control the reward system and sensory processing: the midbrain ventral tegmental area houses dopamine pathways related to reward, [8] while in the back of the brain, the occipital lobes process visual stimuli and the temporal lobes facilitate "hearing, smell, taste, and higher-level visual processing." [9] Also located in the back, the parietal lobes "detect light touch, temperature, pain, vibration, and many other modalities" through the skin. [10] These regions providing sensory processing and reward are thus involved in the print-speech neural network.

The link between speech and reading/writing noted in these studies indicates that we still feel a sense of dialogue even when just reading Plato. This preservation of the dialogic spirit is integral to unlocking the truth through inquiry.

The ins and outs of reading Plato

There are a few things you need to keep in mind when deciding the order in which you want to read Plato. Historical context is important, and you can read on about the events in Plato's life and how they may have affected his work. Literary techniques also factor in, for even though Plato was a philosopher, his dialogues are so well-written that they are read as literature, as well. When it comes to interpretation of the more allegorical material, the sky's the limit. Plato's rich use of literary devices makes reading in thematic order an enticing process.

The best thing about reading Plato thematically is that it allows you to concentrate on the areas you are passionate about, reading them in closer proximity to one another than you might get with a chronological reading. Politically-minded readers will likely enjoy the "Republic" and "Laws," while hopeless romantics may draw inspiration from the "Symposium" and "Phaedrus." Anyone interested in metaphysics (or the nature of things) need look no further than the "Parmenides" and "Timaeus." There are a couple of drawbacks to reading by theme, though: It's harder to see Plato's philosophical/artistic evolution over time, and we also lose the thread on any *historical* progress that influenced personal growth. We can better track these with the chronological approach.

When reading Plato chronologically, we easily see his ideas and writing style evolve over the course of his life. Early, middle, and late works are so grouped because of similarity in structure and content, with early dialogues tending to focus on Socrates and his trial, as with the "Apology" and "Euthyphro," and end in uncertainty about the concept discussed (*aporia*), while middle and later works like "Theaetetus" and "Parmenides" tackled more complex philosophical concepts and featured more conclusive endings. (Both middle and late dialogues favored longer, more thorough discussions, with later works the most intricate.) This approach is more standard but by no means more perfect, for themes and concepts stick less when they are distanced in the ordering. In addition, forcing yourself through other works written in x year just to get to the one you like at y could make for a dry reading experience.

Also, Plato lived a long time ago. Because of this, "most developmentalists [who believe that 'Plato's views evolved significantly throughout his career'] [...] agree that it is impossible to line up Plato's works like pearls on a string and to reconstruct his progress from dialogue to dialogue." [11] Some evidence suggests that he redrafted dialogues throughout his lifetime. Scholars think the first book of the "Republic" was written as a single dialogue long before the rest of it due to shared characteristics with early works, and it might even have been edited so it would better fit the later work on the whole. [12]

These factors complicate *any* ordering of Plato's work. There are so many things to consider, and our order choice sways us into different readings of the same material. Reading Plato the right way (fully engaged regardless of the order used) impacts how closely we relate to his ideas: jumping into the difficult "Parmenides" head-first without any research is a quick way to turn you off the material, and ignoring classic interpretation of the "Republic" by taking allegorical material too literally will surely result in a looser grasp on the work. Picking the right order for you and paying close attention to literary devices and historical context can help guard against these problems.

Action Steps

With the help of this exercise, figure out which order of Plato's works you would like to pursue (i.e., thematic or chronological). Consider:

- If your interest in the dialogues is general or specific
- Whether you prefer a conventional or more creative approach
- Your preferred subject(s): history, philosophy, literature

You can use these basic considerations as a launchpad for others such as research preferences and the knowledge base you are bringing to your reading experience. If your focus is on Plato's life as well as his work, a chronological approach might make sense. Alternatively, if you would like to delve deeply into how each work is structured while noting similarities in other works, the thematic approach might be for you.

Indeed, it can be difficult knowing where to start, but hopefully, the above exercise got you going in the right direction. Learning about the details of his life is also helpful, and you will see in Chapter 2 how Plato grew up during the Peloponnesian War with Cratylus and Socrates for tutors and nurtured political aspirations in his youth.

Chapter Summary

- The thematic approach to reading Plato groups similar works together, such as the "Republic" and "Laws" (politics).

- Chronological ordering is more conventional, but discontinuity from possible redrafting over the years complicates this approach.
- Thematic ordering lets you focus on favorite topics, while reading chronologically can reveal personal and historical progress.

2

YOUTH, WAR, AND SOCRATIC INFLUENCE

WHAT DRIVES THE PATH TO BECOMING A PHILOSOPHER

Plato's clarity and reach into the present stop just short of time travel, highlighting a society still steeped in ancient tradition. The miraculous survival of all his work into the present was no accident, as scholar after scholar found value there, keeping his teachings alive by passing them down.

Plato's ideas stayed in the periphery long after the fall of Greece to Rome in 163 B.C.E. (and the fall of Rome itself in 476 C.E.), even when people couldn't directly access his dialogues. Late into Byzantine (east Roman) rule in the mid-15th century, leading philosopher George Gemistos Plethon ruffled feathers by endorsing Plato over Aristotle who was favored at the time. Plato beat the odds of lost texts and literary career gaps plaguing other great thinkers with whom he brushed elbows, enjoying a near-monopoly over Western philosophy in "later antiquity" that would propel him forward throughout the course of history. [1]

Imagine your favorite rock star. Now imagine people listening to their music two thousand years later. Not many composers or musicians from antiquity are still household names like Plato and his associates Socrates and Aristotle. (Pythagoras gets some credit for inventing the seven-note scale, however.) Classical Greece's chief playwrights remain familiar, but only with a fraction of their body of work still with us. The apparent eagerness to hang onto Plato's every word shows in the survival of his entire oeuvre, an anomaly among most other renowned figures we receive piecemeal.

Two millennia on, Plato's reach over modern culture remains almost universal with tenets that can be applied at any level and pace. One lightly posited theory from Plato's "Laches" dialogue still beckons: that true bravery occurs only when the agent knows the stakes are high and feels some form of dread. [2] Even Shakespeare declared that "cowards die many times before their deaths; the valiant never taste of death but once." [3]

For instance, Plato's "Allegory of the Cave" speaks to anyone who feels or has felt that there is more to life than they are currently experiencing, a dissatisfaction that forms the drive behind many celebrated philosophers' quest for meaning.

Plato found this meaning in Forms (eternal ideals) sometime after they were discussed at Socrates' execution. He also upheld Socrates' stringent principles, showing in his "Crito" dialogue the elder philosopher's famous refusal to escape in favor of obeying the Form of Justice and being put to death as the law dictated. [4] That level of dedication may not be feasible for modern readers.

Still, many of Plato's other ideas are applicable to modern-day thinking. Anyone who wonders about religion or the existence of cosmic order can draw from the above notions about bravery, justice, and the ubiquity of similar tenets. You can boost your natural critical thinking abilities by adopting Plato into your everyday life. Start asking questions, then start asking more, releasing the curiosity of your inner child as Plato did under trusted tutors.

By using inquiry on a solid base of reason, you gain access to knowledge and truth like Plato did. In his case, however, growing up during the Peloponnesian War may have impacted his knowledge acquisition process. Things tend to move faster in wartime, even a child's education. According to some sources, he would be in the thick of it later.

A boy in the midst of war

Athens was overflowing with creative and intellectual innovation in 428-7 B.C.E. at the time of Plato's birth. Playwrights Aeschylus, Sophocles, and Euripides made leaps in dramatic achievement during Greece's Classical Period in the fifth and fourth centuries, and Western philosophy continued to grow. Democracy also advanced during this time, although it was briefly overthrown as you'll read later. [5] This flourishing, followed by a period of flux on the road to tyranny and back again, may have inspired Plato to later identify his Forms as eternal.

Plato grew up in an aristocratic household under parents Ariston and Perictione with three siblings, enjoying a solid political background and an ancestor who was kinsman to Solon, a celebrated Athenian statesman and poet who lived in the sixth century B.C.E. and ruled as archon for a time. Although Plato would never rule Athens, he still had kingship in his blood via one Dropides who was "archon of the year 644 B.C.E." Dropides had a great-great-grandson named Critias who gave his name to an additional grandson who helped topple democracy after the Peloponnesian War. [6] We will return to the latter Critias shortly.

These connections may have informed Plato's interest in politics. [7] He was born during the Peloponnesian War, which arose from a rivalry gone sour with Athens and Sparta fighting over city-states to incorporate into their respective political alliances. This predicted dueling focuses on politics and philosophy and a complicated life, with some accounts placing him as a soldier in the final years of the war. [8] This could have shaped his views on courage chronicled in the early dialogue "Laches," and the brief fall of democracy after the war ended almost certainly predicted his depiction of failing government in the "Republic."

Rewind to the First Peloponnesian War

A prior war, the First Peloponnesian War, broke out about twenty years after the Delian League's formation, [9] and tensions spiked between Athens and Sparta. This dynamic of mounting resentments between two wars in relatively quick succession and the involvement of many city-states evokes similarities between the Peloponnesian Wars and the World Wars to occur about 2,500 years later.

Ending in 445 B.C.E., the First Peloponnesian War brought about a treaty and 14 years of "peace" that unraveled in 433 when Athens broke the treaty's terms through a sneaky alliance with Corcyra (now known as Corfu). At the time, Corinth, a Spartan ally, had claimed Corcyra as a "strategically important" colony, [10] and seizing it was a pointed act of aggression following a brittle truce. Plato would be born just several years before the next conflict began.

Plato and the (Second) Peloponnesian War

Fought between 431 and 404 B.C.E., [11] the second Peloponnesian War began as a rivalry between the Delian League (Athens) and the Peloponnesian League (Sparta). These powerful associations battled for influence over the remaining city-states. The older Peloponnesian League had flourished alone in the sixth century. But when the Delian League was formed in 478, bringing the power of other city-states behind Athens, it emerged as competition for Sparta. [12] Most Greek city-states fell behind either of the two leagues as the rivalry blossomed into war, more change on the horizon for a young Plato.

We don't know exactly what Plato was doing at this time, but the societal flux he had grown up with must have impacted him in his formative years. Certain accounts say he served in the military as a young man from 409 to 404. After democracy was overthrown and then restored, he made strides to enter politics, perhaps thinking that with his background and talents, he would make a good leader where good leadership was clearly necessary. But Socrates' execution five years later would put him off public life for good. [13]

A traitor and two subversive relatives

Before it was defeated, Athens suffered the traitorous actions of a man called Alcibiades who liked to play both sides. Linked to both Socrates as his lover and Plato through multiple inclusions in his dialogues, Alcibiades is almost as renowned as they are, though more for scandal than accomplishment. He was a "brilliant but unscrupulous" Athenian general known for courage and shrewdness who could not always be trusted to use his talents for Athens' benefit. [14] Pushing Athens into a doomed military affair in Sicily and then faced with the death penalty for an unrelated event, Alcibiades promptly defected to Sparta. [15]

After switching sides, Alcibiades switched sides *again* and helped Athens with a successful coup d'état that got him a role commanding the navy. This restored his popularity in his native Athens, and all charges were dropped. [16] But his legacy was forever marred, and modern-day history buffs don't tend to hold him in very high regard. Interestingly, Plato's "Symposium" sidesteps these events despite featuring Alcibiades as a major character. This could be excused by the dialogue's earlier setting, but the avoidance also might have been to avoid awkwardness.

Meanwhile, at the close of the war, two men related to Plato's mother seized power: Critias and Charmides, who participated in a violent takedown of democracy in favor of oligarchical rule. [17] These figures might have directly inspired Plato's discussion about government in the "Republic," where the convergence of family and politics appears to have had a complicated effect on Plato's work. His biting summation of tyranny implied an aversion to the tactics his relatives took, although he himself would later condemn democracy as a mere step above tyranny.

Unfortunately, it was tyranny that Athens would soon be battling. The city selected a group, the Thirty Tyrants, to govern the city upon Sparta's instruction. But the Thirty were after their own ends, determined to swap out democracy with a more self-serving oligarchy and aiming to "reform" society by changing laws that they did not agree with—and eliminating or exiling people they similarly found disagreeable. [18] Their bloody regime lasted just eight months but drastically changed Athenian life during that period, creating chaos in the city.

Though met with little resistance at first, the Thirty Tyrants eventually attracted discontentment for their cruelty toward anyone who did not share their vision.

Better ideas were in high demand, which might have spurred Plato on in his political ambition (as well as later in his philosophical work). Democratic rule was restored in 403 after some of the exiled launched a counterattack at Phyle. [19] Those displaced got their property back, and those of the Thirty who were still alive had to stay in Eleusis: coming back to Athens meant submitting to an investigation. [20]

Plato named tyranny as the worst form of government in the "Republic" and wanted to try out politics for himself after democracy returned, which indicates a lack of satisfaction with the leadership he witnessed. One could go as far as to interpret his political earnestness as making sure Athens never saw such decay again.

It's easy to imagine that Plato's contributions to political philosophy and musings on a perfect society were in direct response to the messy, ever-changing Athens he had experienced in the Peloponnesian War, as he alluded to in the "Seventh Letter." No one writes about utopia without desiring change, and some of his more radical ideas (like raising children in common to better prepare them for kingship) speak to a world so imperfect that radical changes were needed.

The dark period close to the end of the war fueled demand for a different, more enlightened approach, and Plato himself would later explore the reaching implications of power in "The Republic."

This dialogue is a fundamental text of Western philosophy, which was still in its infancy when Plato arrived on the scene and worked his way up to become its most recognized figure. Building on the work of pre-Socratics like Heraclitus, Plato introduced the world to Forms, the Socratic Method, and a concrete answer to why we should act ethically. These ideas may have originated with Socrates but were certainly popularized through Plato's decision to write them down and teach them at his Academy. He drew from a perfect storm of ambition and access to the best thinkers in Greece, for it was claimed none was wiser than Socrates, as we'll see in the "Apology" in Chapter 3. Having lived so long ago, Plato and his contemporaries still had much to discover; his keen mind shaped him into one of ancient Greece's first (and best) philosophical pioneers.

Feeding a keen mind

According to Aristotle, Plato had found an early tutor in Cratylus, and in turn, Cratylus had been a follower of famed pre-Socratic philosopher Heraclitus. Scholars sometimes question this anecdotal source, but Cratylus probably taught him the Heraclitean doctrine: the idea that the only constant is constant change. This fascinated Plato for the rest of his life. [21]

Plato's Theory of Forms responded to the Heraclitean doctrine by pinpointing overarching concepts that did *not* change in contrast to their smaller, more corporeal counterparts that did. (Love as a notion is static, for example, whereas individual manifestations of it are in flux.)

Socrates' mentorship had an even greater effect on Plato. The elder philosopher eschewed writing down his lectures, one habit that Plato did not share (if he had, who knows if we would ever have heard of either of them)? Yet Socrates' silence on the page just created more space and demand for Plato's doting dialogues featuring his tutor, passed down generations into modern knowledge.

In fact, Plato's dialogue format is arguably his greatest innovation. Through it, he spread the informed ideas of Socrates or, in Cratylus's case, riffed on them. Discussion-based classes continue to serve as a cornerstone of university education over two thousand years later.

Following Cratylus, Socrates became Plato's greater focus, sometimes to Plato's own exclusion. Some have even identified Socrates as a mouthpiece through which Plato could assert his own ideas.

Plato did have his own ideas, though, writing things down while Socrates deliberately didn't. Still, his lifelong dedication to Socrates suggests some level of fidelity to his historical legacy, even if his own philosophical prowess indicated a drive for independent flexibility. Most agree that his depiction is partly historical portrayal and partly personal mouthpiece.

Socrates features in most of Plato's dialogues, and given how closely their lives overlapped in history, some see the two philosophers as ideologically interchangeable. A few additionally turn to the more rebellious Aristotle to highlight the similarity between Socrates' and Plato's ideas. However, grouping the first two philosophers as interchangeable is a reductionist approach and leaves no room for nuance. Unlike Socrates, Plato had interests other than philosophy, to wit, politics.

Having varied interests may have been wise, given that not all ideas were popular. Socrates' trial left Plato shaken, and following his teacher's execution, Plato left Athens for Megara, where the philosopher Euclides could offer some protection. [22] This much is corroborated by Hermodorus. Plato is known to have traveled to Italy at 40 and possibly Cyrene and Egypt in addition. He would have been around 29 at the time of Socrates' execution and founded his Academy, promptly upon return to Athens, in about 387 while in his early forties. [23] That made for a little over a decade of travel, if indeed he had been traveling all that time.

No expiration on Plato's ideas

Plato's ideas still speak to us. His early and middle works endorse true bravery and leading with reason in thought, which continues to provide value to those wishing to develop critical thinking skills.

Early works often ended in indecision, and the "Laches" was no exception, failing to pinpoint exactly what bravery was. Backtracking in the text, however, revealed that bravery was knowing the risks and acting anyway, a sentiment with which many modern readers vibe.

In contrast to early works, Plato's middle works offered longer, more conclusive arguments. The "Republic" asserted that the soul was to be led by reason, not emotion or baser appetites. "The just and honorable action…[is] that which preserves and helps to produce the condition of soul," he claimed, "and wisdom the science that presides over such conduct." [24]

Late works are the most intricate of all, whether it's a treatment of how a craftsman deity created the universe as explored in the "Timaeus" or a labyrinthine deep dive into the origin and nature of laws in Plato's dialogue of the same name. Other works from this period include the "Critias," "Sophist," and "Philebus." [25]

Plato's "Allegory of the Cave" from the "Republic" enjoyed such renown that it would cross over into literary works such as *Fahrenheit 451:* Ray Bradbury directly cited the allegory with characters "like gray animals peering from electronic caves, faces with gray colorless eyes." [26] As we will later see in Plato's Cave, Plato likened humans to a group of people in a cave gazing at shadows on the wall they are chained to [27] and discussed them exiting the cave into the light, thought to be akin to learning the truth about what's real and what isn't. "[The cave dweller] would be able to look upon the sun itself and see its true nature," declared Plato through Socrates, "not by reflections in water or phantasms of it in an alien setting, but in and by itself in its own place." [28]

Think about the times in your life when you felt you were living on a higher setting. Ideals are subjective, and Plato's Forms are adaptable for anyone who finds value in "next stepping" into a better life. Seeking wisdom, Plato believed, is the only way to find it: All it takes to put yourself in the cave scenario is a mild sensory deprivation, something to cast shadows, and time. You can find a more detailed sensory deprivation exercise at the beginning of Chapter 6. If you want to try leading in reason, simply opt out of the next temptation you know you can't control (like bingeing on chocolate or Netflix).

The way Plato thought is already similar to ways we moderns think, at least in some ways. We are all human, and to be human is to enjoy the reach of our working minds. And modern thinkers need not go to Athens to access Plato's wisdom. Plato's writings (and good information about them) can easily be found on the Internet. His legacy courses through the art of critical thinking today, and a few of his ideas may sound familiar to you.

Here philosophy and psychology converge. Consider this US study on conforming habits which tasked 28 volunteers with choosing and rating songs they liked and wanted to own. During an fMRI a week later, they were directed to rate songs and profiles of two "expert reviewers," with an average rating of 4 out of 7 indicating that most valued the reviewers' opinions. Later on, participants were offered a token for one of these songs (the ten most popular of which they'd be given) to further incentivize choices. [29]

When the token they received was for a song chosen by both reviewers, the participants were happier, with the fMRI unearthing a link between this pattern and "more blood oxygenation level-dependent (**BOLD**) activity in the ventral striatum [which contains the mesolimbic dopamine pathway]," implying reward. [30]

In this example, concepts stand in as valued objects like the songs promised to the participants, and reward for choosing what those more qualified have selected speaks not just to conformity but to the calling of a more refined knowledge base.

Just like the participants flocked to the reviewers' choices, we continue to flock to Plato's ideas over two thousand years after his death. Less than a hundred years ago, authors were still sampling his allegorical work and continue to do so today. Modern philosophers layer innumerable interpretations over his dialogues to the point of granting him new life. Plato has been bending people's ears since his youth, attracting converts with his reverence for the unchanging Forms. And over and over again, his ideas have been adopted, reimagined, and carried to new listeners.

Action Steps

Asking Questions

1. Take three sheets of paper and grab a pen.
2. On the first sheet, write down the first broad concept that interests you (intelligence, peace, etc.).
3. On the second sheet, write down as many questions about the concept as you can think of. Don't stop to answer each one just yet. They need not be deep inquiries; even mundane questions can yield surprising insights. Once you've assembled three to five questions, move on to the next step.
4. Answer each question on the third sheet of paper, taking as much time as you need to thoroughly address them.
5. Returning to the first sheet, write down at least one example and one quality of your concept based on what you have learned or other observations. (Examples may be specific instances, but qualities must describe the entire concept. Rectangular describes all squares and can be considered a quality. A red square, on the other hand, serves as an example.)

All this may take longer than expected, but don't rush yourself. Developing your own sense of curiosity is essential to learning to think like Plato. Good ideas come more quickly with other brains involved, as you'll see in the next exercise.

Asking Questions with Friends

1. Take yourself through all the steps above with at least one other person, speaking instead of writing things down. The back-and-forth will take you to places you didn't expect!

Moving On

The sharp jut of Plato's ideas into today's world really does start to look like time travel if you recall the old adage: The more things change, the more they stay the same. Though our world looks quite different, we still think in time-trodden traditions about reason, love, bravery, and because of this, Plato's ideas will never go out of fashion as long as humans are alive.

Chapter Summary

- In Plato's youth, he was tutored by Cratylus, who taught him the Heraclitean Principle.
- Plato met Socrates as a young man and became his devoted student.
- Plato grew up with the Peloponnesian War and was related to two of the Thirty Tyrants who briefly overthrew Athenian democracy after it ended.
- Athens' political climate likely inspired Plato's discussion of government in the "Republic."

- We tend to flock to the same universal concepts over time, as Plato's lasting popularity shows.

3

THE TRIAL

WHAT WONDERMENT AND A WISE MENTOR
CAN DO FOR OUR PURSUIT OF TRUTH

Plato spoke of weeping at Socrates' deathbed. [1] Although the Athenians had sentenced him to death for corrupting the youth (he didn't), he did not greet death with dread. One onlooker in the "Phaedo" is young Phaedo, who was formerly enslaved but gained freedom through an associate of Socrates and went on to become one of his acolytes. [2] His and the others' weeping was distinctive amidst Socrates' calm and Plato's endorsement of leading with reason and letting feelings follow. Here, crying was communal and appropriate, even if Socrates shamed them for it. [3]

In fact, ancient Greeks often hired professional grievers. Professional grieving still exists in some areas of the world today, [4] validating the sharing of feelings during difficult times. Such public displays, however uncomfortable, can bond people together. Sometimes it's as simple as seeing someone look the way you feel, even if you've been trying to hide it.

The weepers in Plato's work were men, packing an extra punch given the social repercussions men still sometimes face just for crying. Keeping things in is the alternative, but repression isn't good for you: A 2012 meta-analysis of 22 studies on repressive coping noted "significant associations between repressive coping, cancer, and cardiovascular diseases, especially hypertension." [5] Although cancer-focused studies were most numerous at 45%, repression is also associated with less devastating illnesses like asthma and diabetes. Researchers examined health data from 6,775 participants, looking for a link between signs of repression and these illnesses. Repression could be seen in heart rate variability, or the gap between two heartbeats, which differed from those who didn't repress "in a pathological direction and that is predictive for cardiac problems." [6]

The meta-analysis found a steep risk (80%) that repressors will have higher blood pressure than "nonrepressors." [7] Other results were less conclusive, recalling the "chicken and egg dilemma" of whether repression caused cancer or cancer repression. (Only two studies looked at repression *before* the diagnosis, making this difficult to answer). [8] In any case, repression is bad for you, and the ancients' normalization of grief expression does much to support people today who may feel boxed in.

Several of Socrates' friends wept at his deathbed. However, the unfazed philosopher had accepted his fate by the end of the "Apology" and chastised them for grieving him. Whether or not Plato was present among his friends is unclear, but he made his own feelings clear in the "Seventh Letter" (quoted later in the chapter) in which he spoke of being so appalled by Socrates' trial and execution that he quit his political aspirations. And if Hermodorus is right about him skipping town afterward, that may be telling enough.

Thanks to the "Republic," Plato is known for his reason-regulating-all approach. However, his earnest portrayal of grief being expressed also honors appropriate shows of feeling, which sounds more encouraging to those who wear their heart on their sleeve.

Socrates' death in 399 B.C.E. impacted Plato and his desire to form his own school, especially because the two philosophers shared so many ideas by dint of their close friendship and teacher-student relationship. Plato's "Apology" chronicles his tutor's defense and demise with a solemnity that predicts the impact of Socrates' execution on Plato's philosophy. After shifting his focus to Forms, Plato might have seen Athenian democracy differently.

These developments forever changed the trajectory of Western thought. Plato's overall fidelity to Socrates' teachings would pave the way for his own pupil, Aristotle, to diverge and rebel. And the concepts stuck; these three are the most recognizable faces of ancient philosophy today.

Socrates and Plato: The thinker's bond

At the time of his execution Socrates was already elderly, a plea he makes in the "Apology." [9] He was considered somewhat of a nuisance among the Athenians for his philosophical approach. For one thing, he would go up to people and start deep conversations with them, just assuming that they are willing to take part in such a discussion.

Socrates took this tactic all the way up until his trial. (The "Euthyphro" depicts a discussion occurring just before.) For another, he would hold back and pretend not to know anything, which conversants did not appreciate, even if Socrates believed that letting them discover ideas for themselves was better for them. It's safe to say that Socrates wasn't a popular character at the time of his trial, but he did much more for his native city than annoy them.

Famously, Socrates asserted: "The unexamined life is not worth living." He took this curiosity to great lengths over many decades, almost to a fault. One of his most enduring ideas is that true knowledge is admitting to what a person doesn't know, a theme found in the "Apology."

While the "Apology" focused on the trial, the "Phaedo" that took place afterward featured the first known discussion of Plato's Theory of Forms. In it, Plato imbued his characterization of Socrates with belief in these Forms as he lay dying; for knowledge of them, Socrates claimed, is born to us. Recollection comes from innate familiarity with these universal concepts: Upon experiencing a real-life manifestation of a Form, it is the latter by which you recognize it. [10] For example, falling in love with a specific person is recognizable by a broad understanding of what love is.

Scholars distinguish between a Form and an instance of it occurring with capital and lowercase letters (Form vs. form, Love vs. love), making it easy to follow the thread from one to the other in your critical thinking. The Theory of Forms will be further explained in Chapter 4.

If Forms are Plato's trademark, beginning with Socrates but developing far beyond his lifetime, then Socrates' inquiry technique is *his* trademark asset. The Socratic Method consisted of a discussion facilitating questions and answers on a certain concept (or object) that was meant to unearth revelations about the qualities of the concept. Although many were willing to participate in the discussion, others became frustrated. In fact, the *Republic* opens with Thrasymachus getting belligerent over his stated opinion that might equals right. [11]

Socrates did not write down his lectures, believing that too much would be lost without dialogue. The novelty of distinct minds and the intuition beneath spoken words made for better discourse in his mind.

Plato's Socrates character can be as frustrating as the Athenians found the real man. His method included a healthy dose of "dissembling," or holding back information to elicit it from another through dialogue instead, because in a teaching context, he relied on students discovering his natural discoveries for themselves. Plato and others referred to this dissembling as "insincerity," or *eirôneia*. [12]

Socrates felt that this type of insincerity was integral to good teaching, given he was always several steps ahead of his students and didn't want to make things too easy for them. It was a way of ensuring that what they learned stuck. Plato noted his approach of holding back in the "Apology," "Republic," and "Symposium."

This approach, however effective it proved, still tends to drive readers up the wall. Though Socrates' execution was undoubtedly excessive, some of the ire directed his way is understandable. Patience is a virtue… especially when reading Platonic dialogues.

Additional patience is needed in piecing together Socrates' life, with much still unknown due to his not writing anything down. He was born and died in Athens, the son of Sophroniscus and Phaenarete. (He had three sons in turn). [13] Additionally, he was a hoplite (citizen-soldier) during the Peloponnesian War, and Plato placed him in Potidaea in 432 B.C.E., a northern city-state that wanted to secede from the Athenian alliance. (Think the American South in the Civil War). [14]

Shortly afterward, Socrates "saved the life and armour of Alcibiades" during an ambush, beginning their acquaintance. [15] His engagement at Podiaea during the Peloponnesian War lasted three years, and in 424,

Socrates fought the Boeotians in central Greece in the Battle of Delium, where a friendly fire fatality occurred for the first time on record.

At this time Socrates was in his mid-forties, hardly the young man Plato had been when he had served in the same war. Yet after Sparta roundly defeated Athens at Amphipolis in 422, the Athenian general Laches, who lent his name to one of Plato's dialogues, worked in some praise amidst lamentation: "If all the Athenians had fought as bravely as Socrates, the Boeotians would have erected no [victory] statues." [16]

Socrates distinguished himself not only as a soldier but a lover, as well. He and Alcibiades knew each other for about twelve to fifteen years when Plato chronicled their romantic relationship in the "Symposium." He would even try his hand at philosophy in this dialogue, although Plato ultimately made a better student to Socrates.

Living with Socrates' absence must have been difficult for Plato. Assuming that Plato met him by age 25, he would have been a close associate for at least two years, and his dedication to preserving his teacher's legacy is evident in the creation of the Academy after his death.

As his most eminent student, Plato took many of his teacher's ideas for his own. This, in large part, is why we even know his name.

Socrates' doomed trial

The Athenians had finally grown sick of the Socratic Method, complaining that he was corrupting the youth and spreading atheism. Comic playwrights, including Aristophanes, piled on by lampooning Socrates' poor reputation in Athens, which, cited directly in the trial, led to his downfall.

Socrates' enemies also believed him to be a sophist: someone who was a master in persuasion and used rhetoric to make any argument, no matter how unpopular.

This, plus the habitual dissembling Plato noted, caused Athenians to think that Socrates was using his intellect to teach false notions. In their minds, he was teaching youth to disrespect their elders, and therefore they charged him with corrupting the youth. [17]

But very little of the "evidence" they brought has stuck over the last two and a half thousand years. Socrates is no longer identified as a sophist or an atheist, and nor has he achieved martyr status despite fitting the bill. Yet his gadfly reputation *did* persist, giving occasionally frustrated modern readers an idea of why Athens had a bone to pick with him.

Despite any shortcomings in his approach, Socrates' ideas are his legacy. Plato has done him service by making his dialogues readable under a literary lens as well as a philosophical one, portraying Socrates lovingly as a character while noting his shortcomings (related to insincerity). As a result, Socrates is still talked about and appreciated.

Socrates was 70 years old in 399, [18] and considering that Plato lived until about 80 [19] and the playwright Sophocles 90, [20] it seems clear that Socrates, though elderly, was not yet approaching a natural death. His defense speech, though calm, breathed urgent sincerity.

We glean most of what we know from the dialogues surrounding the trial, particularly the "Apology." Plato's Socrates started off the "Apology" by making clear that he was not accustomed to political speech and that the accusers, while well-spoken, were lying about him. [21]

A prosecutor named Meletus brought the charges. [22] Xenophon claims Meletus negotiated peace with the Lacedaemonians when the Thirty Tyrants were in power, [23] though little else is known of him, establishing direct tension between him and Socrates through the treachery of Alcibiades. Through Socrates, Plato painted Meletus as "pretending to be zealous and concerned about things on which he never cared at all." [24] Hence a very different type of insincerity.

Socrates indelicately informed the assembly that according to the Oracle (the priestess interpreting Apollo at Delphi), no one was wiser than he. [25] Himself disbelieving this, he set out to find wiser people but found that they all professed knowledge that they could not actually have known. Upon pointing out to them that they were mistaken in their claim on wisdom, not perhaps deliberately dishonest but surely not thinking things through, Socrates upset them, decreasing his popularity as he burned through "wise man" after "wise man" in the territory. [26] Afterward, he took true wisdom to mean being forthcoming about knowing very little at all. [27]

In the "Apology," Socrates remarked that idle, rich young men would journey with him as he continued seeking out the wiser in the days before the trial, and he said that they would "find pleasure in hearing people being examined, and often imitate me themselves, and then they [would] undertake to examine others." [28] Less impressed were their fathers, who raised the alarm about Socrates "corrupting" their children. (Sound familiar?)

In the courtroom, Socrates attempted to engage Meletus in a cooperative dialogue regarding his guilt. Meletus at first was silent, necessitating that Socrates answer himself, [29] which of course, slashed the efficacy of his method. When he edged Meletus into reluctant responses, he was finally able to argue that he *did* believe in gods and spirits and was uninterested in corrupting anyone. [30]

Socrates saw that public opinion was against him, and he predicted his condemnation [31] but without dread or fear of death. He cited Achilles' bravery [32] and explained that fear of death was another instance of false wisdom, as no one knows what happens after death. [33] Later on in the "Crito," he even declined a friend's attempt to break him out of jail.

Given the chance to stop his philosophizing and go free, Socrates admitted that he would not do so. [34] Championing his gadfly image, he asserted, "If you put me to death, you will not easily find another." [35]

Socrates lost 30 votes away from being acquitted. [36] Following the verdict, he still insisted that he did no wrong but chose death over exile, [37] and he implored others to continue his work for his three sons, "troubling them as I have troubled you" (in other words, making them think and stirring up cobwebbed assumptions). [38]

He died after drinking hemlock shortly afterward.

Plato up to bat

Socrates' trial and execution created a ripple effect for philosophers, and we have traces of information about how Plato reacted. He might have left Athens in fear for himself, but Herodotus may have exaggerated this claim. Based on Plato's writings and what we know about Socrates, however, the latter's influence on the former is undeniable.

The "Seventh Letter," attributed to Plato due to stylistic similarities with his dialogues (although someone else may have written it), harbors his feelings about Athens' political climate and Socrates' treatment within it: "I imagined that they would administer the State by leading it out of an unjust way of life into a just way, and consequently I gave my mind to them very diligently," Plato wrote. "And indeed I saw how these men within a short time caused men to look back on the former government as a golden age; and above all how they treated my aged friend Socrates." [39]

Plato cited two instances where he got put off his political calling, both related to Socrates. First, the politicians tried to get Socrates to bring a citizen before them to be put to death, and Socrates refused to his peril. "So when I beheld all these actions and others of a similar grave kind," Plato claimed, "I was indignant, and I withdrew myself from the evil practices then going on." [40]

Then, stirred to eradicate the injustices he had witnessed, Plato would feel the political calling again. But Socrates' execution shortly afterward would disavow him of such aspirations permanently.

"Then once again I was really, though less urgently, impelled with a desire to take part in public and political affairs," he declared. "Many deplorable events, however, were still happening in those times [...] But, as ill-luck would have it, certain men of authority summoned our comrade Socrates before the law-courts, laying a charge against him which was most unholy, and which Socrates of all men least deserved; for it was on the charge of impiety that those men summoned him and the rest condemned and slew him." [41]

Any person of even middling moral standing would balk at some of the things politicians do. Plato's dueling impulses between good stewardship and good principle, and his strong admiration of Socrates, need no further justification.

Socrates wanted a world where people would "trouble" his three sons when they were adults (along with the young men who had followed him around as symbolic sons), upsetting what they thought they knew to highlight what they didn't. His death formed a springboard for philosophers to continue questioning traditional beliefs, except this time, it would involve too many of them to put to death.

Xenophon also wrote multiple dialogues featuring Socrates that are extant, [42] joined by historian and philosopher Cicero a few centuries later. His dialogues run more Aristotelian in content, however, [43] and examples from other philosophers are lost.

Almost every dialogue Plato wrote (over two dozen) featured Socrates, providing extensive insight into his personality, approach, life, and work. Socrates did not write down any of his lectures, explaining Plato's zealousness.

Ironically, Socrates' wrongful execution catapulted him to a greater level of renown than he ever received in his lifetime, and his death ensured the survival of his name into the present. Gadflies the world over continue eliciting great truths from one another through spoken dialogue, enjoying Socrates as a household name.

In fact, a 2010 study on students asking their teacher questions shows that student questions influence the teacher's approach so that both can better understand one another. [44] The study appraised the usefulness of dialogue in classroom settings by observing two teaching sequences across three science classes in a Brazilian public school associated with the Federal University of Minas Gerais, one in 7th grade and two in 9th, to appraise the usefulness of dialogue in classroom settings. Students were mixed in academic ability and "mainly from a poor social background" but were, on the whole, very interested in their science coursework. [45] In addition, the students were comfortable enough with their teacher to interject with a question.

"In both lessons a limited number of students raised wonderment questions," said the study, "but many other students participated in the discussion initiated by these questions. In some cases, the teacher just answered the question; in other cases, she gave the question back to the class and, most frequently, she addressed the theme of the question calling for contributions from other students." [46]

In the 7th-grade lesson, one student asked for additional information beyond the scope of the discussion, which the teacher welcomed and answered with a narrative. The authors identified this as "interactive/authoritative" in comparison to the more egalitarian "dialogic," with length of narrative being the defining factor: in "interactive/authoritative" discussion, the teacher does most of the talking for a longer period while fielding interjections from students, and the "dialogic" approach consists of shorter speeches from students responding primarily to each other and peripherally the teacher.

The two 9th-grade lessons differ significantly from the 7th-grade lesson. When a student asked a complex question in the first 9th-grade class, the teacher first tried interactive/dialogic communication but eventually gave the question back to the class with a more dialogic approach, refraining from "evaluative comments." [47]

The authors put a spin on their tactics with the second 9th-grade class, this time focusing on student questions addressed to peers rather than to the teacher. A student raised a contesting question, disagreeing not with the teacher but with the ideas covered. In the student discussion, another student took on the more conventional teacher approach with "long turns of speech and some evaluative comments." [48] When additional questions delayed the task completion, tension between these two students arose. Although there was some mimicking of the "interactive/authoritative" model, the overall pattern was dialogic. [49]

Why do hierarchies tend to arise in class discussions? The path to a dialogic approach seems more difficult than it first appears. The authors mused that "the stance of the student in asking questions in the science classroom might also represent a search for an authoritative voice, the attempt to master an authorized point of view, which is scientific public knowledge." [50] This describes knowledge acquisition to a tee. They concluded that the interaction itself, rather than the teacher controls dialogic discussion, placing the onus on participants and their level of engagement.

Desiring authority in knowledge acquisition is what Socrates was all about, spending his life in pursuit of such authority, although his ease of manner in the dialogues suggests that he came to possess it in his later years. His ideas are certainly nuanced enough.

Though Plato is easy to read, the arguments he shares from Socrates can be difficult to digest. This has scholars arguing over anything from the intended meaning to the practicality of implementing his ideas, with the plurality of debate giving readers the opportunity to read the same work under multiple distinct lenses.

Few known philosophers inspire such depth of study as Plato does. His layered ideas appeal to a wide crowd, and he is an indispensable inclusion on nearly every philosophy and literature class reading list. Readers of Plato will find that their minds have opened to more possibilities than they ever could have imagined.

Action Steps

Found An Academy

Plato founded an academy around the Socratic Method and wrote dialogues commemorating his teacher.

1. Think about what knowledge you would like to impart to your students. Narrow down your ideas to two and write them down on a new sheet of paper.
2. Start figuring out how you would like to teach. To cover the three different types of learning, flip your paper over and create three columns. Label them "Visual," "Auditory," and "Kinesthetic."

3. Draw one example of visual aid for each idea. For example, if "An apple a day keeps the doctor away!" is one of your tenets, a picture of an apple would suffice.
4. In the next column, repeat this step for auditory learning. Drawing sounds may be difficult, so words, songs, and mnemonics may be written in. ("The early bird gets the worm," may be designated by birdsong or whistling.)
5. Finally, repeat this step for kinesthetic learning. This one will be the hardest. To get started, think of a simple movement for the aphorism "What goes around comes around."

The two chief steps of operating a Platonic Academy are thinking and talking. Did any of the learning mode steps create new insights or subtly change the way you thought about your ideas? As a bonus, talk through your ideas with friends and/or family in a dialogue.

Moving On

Plato's portrayal of men weeping in the *Phaedo* and his impassioned "Seventh Letter" (if he wrote it) add an emotional component to Socrates' trial and execution, helping modern readers contextualize the gravity behind these events for philosophers of the day… and even now.

Chapter Summary

- The Socratic Method encourages asking and answering questions in a dialogue setting to better understand a concept.
- Socrates stood trial for corrupting the youth. A group of Athenians thought he was teaching them to disrespect their elders.
- During his trial, Socrates asserted that he was wise because he didn't pretend to possess knowledge he didn't have.
- Plato included Socrates as a character in almost all his dialogues.
- Plato built his Academy sometime after Socrates was condemned to death in 399 B.C.E.

4

DISTANT IDEALS NO MORE

WHAT IS PLATO'S THEORY OF FORMS AND HOW
DO THEY SHAPE OUR PERCEPTIONS

Socrates, in prison, declined rescue from his friend in Plato's "Crito," with reasoning that was equally intriguing and frustrating. Crito of Alopece, an agriculturalist and Socrates' longtime friend, [1] told Socrates that he and his friends would bribe the guards and care for Socrates after helping him escape. Aside from noting that the philosopher would be abandoning his kids by staying put to die, he implored that he would "lose a friend such as I can never find again." He complained that if he left without Socrates, it would look like he hadn't tried hard enough to persuade him. [2] Though his anguish is sincere, he clearly also wanted Socrates to come with him to settle his own peace of mind.

Crito got Socrates to admit that justice had erred in putting him to death, but Socrates argued that he still had to obey the general Form of Justice by respecting human law, even where it failed him. [3] This meant weathering his death sentence and sending Crito home empty-handed after he ran out of arguments to sway Socrates with.

Here rises a tension between justice and Justice, for most, including Crito, would see nothing wrong with breaking out of an unfair sentence. It is satisfyingly self-serving here to believe that two wrongs *do* make a right. After all, if he shouldn't have been there… why be there?

However, Socrates felt that skipping out on his death sentence would be a betrayal of that which is true and never errs, and his duty to Justice and its perfection as a Form outweighed any indignation at wrongful death. For better or worse, he set aside feelings in favor of sound reasoning as he always did.

Of course, it feels a bit Herculean to act based on a remote ideal rather than the circumstances surrounding you. Not everyone possesses Socrates' superhuman sangfroid, but anyone can aspire to it through reasonable discipline and patience.

The distinction between justice and Justice embodies Plato's Theory of Forms, concepts that were debated during Socrates' final hours (chronicled in the "Phaedo"). He defined Forms as unchanging and eternal ideas that stand behind various similar (but perishable) forms in the world of living things, leading Plato to theorize that the human soul, like Forms, is immortal.

Plato would further argue that philosophy's overall goal was to gain freedom from the limits of physical existence (a thread he would follow with the "Cave Allegory" in the "Republic"; see Chapter 6). Invisible Forms offer "something more" to the right kind of thinker, including the comfort of changeless tenets.

Studying death and immortality

Although set on the day of Socrates' death in 399, the "Phaedo" is attributed to Plato's undated middle period, which also included the "Euthydemus," "Parmenides," "Republic," and "Symposium." [4] Like Plato's other works during this time, the "Phaedo" offered more certainty and clarity regarding posited topics instead of the muddled bemusement found in his early dialogues.[5] This well served the abstraction of Plato's Forms.

Phaedo was Socrates' student, and the eponymous dialogue is centered on his point of view with other speakers including Echecrates, Cebes, Simmias, Crito, and of course, Socrates. His and Plato's Theory of Forms materialized during and after Socrates' death.

The indeterminate gap between his execution and the writing of the "Phaedo" made for a rich, thorough discussion regarding Forms and whether they proved that the soul was immortal. This must have been a fitting comfort for Socrates in his last moments, and it made what could have been a tedious death sequence more engaging.

One of Plato's longer dialogues, the "Phaedo," offers multiple arguments instead of focusing on one. In following the "Apology" and "Crito," as well as the "Euthyphro" just prior to his trial, one major distinction is apparent. The "Phaedo" was likely written later, which means 1) it ended with a conclusive argument rather than uncertainty, 2) the advantage of hindsight applied, and 3) it would more naturally tie into works he had written and would later write.

Though careful not to endorse abandoning the gods, as Socrates was accused of doing, Plato's devotion to the Forms tended to follow a more secular path. The connection between Forms and their worldly counterparts (Beauty and beauty, for example) would place emphasis firmly on human observational faculties, as most, perhaps all, of Plato's ideas relate closely to the human spirit.

Plato's Forms are not merely eternal but understood to be perfect, as well, a perfection Socrates cited in his refusal as the "rightness" of Justice he could not ignore. [6] This rightness would form a key ingredient not only in the "Phaedo" but also in the "Republic," another work from Plato's middle period.

Forms comprised the basis of knowledge and our grasp on reality, Plato said via his Recollection Argument in the "Phaedo," our knowledge of Forms derives from seeing their real-world manifestations, i.e., a pretty woman leads the mind to Aphrodite, goddess of love and beauty. This he referred to as "recollection," with the understanding that all worldly knowledge thus recalls (or leads to) the very concepts that are endemic to human life.

Observation spurs these recollections, and rather than relying on the depth of one idea, Plato here focuses on connections between multiple ideas, an approach modern readers may find much less daunting. The novelty of others' ideas and experiences in dialogue also guarantees good general coverage of human existence.

The first of his middle works, the "Phaedo" is not quite as renowned as other middle works such as the "Republic" and "Symposium," but it remains indispensable both in tracking Plato's ideas over his lifetime and measuring the impact of Socrates' death, at least among his closest friends. Many ideas there also show up in other works, molding an inextricability that, like perfect Justice to Socrates, cannot be ignored.

The world of Forms

Before Plato, Heraclitus and other pre-Socratic philosophers debated the tenor of change. Parmenides claimed, "From nothing, nothing comes," theorizing that the world must have always existed and would continue to exist. Plato tamed these radical concepts, packaging them into something that made sense and resonated with his students and readers.

As stated in the previous section, Forms play a large role in our physical world, for most of what we see, hear, and touch has a flawless, eternal, changeless Form attached to it, according to Plato, even if it hasn't been named yet.

The chief distinction between Forms and forms is physical: one is ethereal while the other is corporeal, and Love, Justice, Bravery, and Piety are not normally things we can touch. However, a brave *person* or a pious *book* can be touched, felt, and understood, allowing us to color in what we don't understand with what we observe.

Understanding the Forms does not come easily due to their incorporeal nature, but Plato's middle works do a wonderful job of providing a roadmap that leads to a general comprehension, if not a complete one. His emphasis that Forms are more real than the physical world creates a noteworthy difficulty for readers: How can we justify following abstractions if we can sense nothing beyond the physical, and what do these abstractions–the Forms–matter in the physical world? (They create steadfastness in an ever-changing realm, but this isn't immediately apparent.)

The intuitiveness of Plato's Recollection Argument might help foster faith in Forms, as the suggestion that we recall concepts based on what we experience might partially explain why these concepts exist in the first place. Even though the Forms exist outside human control, they remain exclusive to human observation, allowing our rational faculties to create an intimacy between ourselves and what we see.

Plato's Forms answered the Problem of Universals, or the possibility of conflating a singular general concept with its many specific iterations: one being many and many, one. (The going theory was that one could not be many and, therefore, that universals uniting multiple forms did not exist.) According to Plato, Forms existed independently of and were superior to the forms associated with them. [7]

The incorporeal-corporeal divide aided with this claim, even if the recollection argument seemed to imply a connection. Perhaps more helpful was Plato's proclamation that no one could possess knowledge regarding anything changeable.

This would mean we cannot say we know the sky is blue because it changes colors. (Both "The sky changes colors" or "The sky is blue at this exact moment in time" would form more appropriate knowledge.) Relating closely to

Socrates' admission that he does not pretend to know any more than he does in the "Apology," Plato's condemnation of "knowledge" around what is changeable cautions us to be very sure of what we know and *can* know.

Plato's specifying what knowledge was both 1) solved the Problem of Universals and 2) limited true knowledge to the unchanging Forms. For many, the immaculateness of his argument outweighed any impracticality of believing in what we could not see or sense, and the possibility of an immortal soul outlined in the "Phaedo" became too tempting to ignore.

Although the physical world reflects the Forms, only the latter is knowable according to Plato. Yet knowing the Forms gives us an understanding that there is much more to what we experience in the world, and the reality is not what we see.

Understanding the soul

The "Phaedo" offers an idea of the soul that differs somewhat from the religious concept, but they share an assertion that the soul is undying. However, Plato's soul operates more as an animating principle: that which makes us alive and may or may not be attached to belief in a deity.

In the first section, a short exchange between Phaedo and Echecrates following Socrates' execution recounted his final words on death and the soul. [8] In this retelling,

Socrates pontificated that death extricated the soul from the body so that each of them existed by themselves. [9] He elected to "turn away from the body and concern himself with the soul," [10] as Plato would later direct his students to do by encouraging them to ignore their distracting, continual appetites for food and sex. This meant recognizing the truth of physical perception as imperfect, with the body's needs proving a distraction. [11]

From here, Socrates redirected his supporters to the truth found in concepts: the only way to gain knowledge about the Forms, he said, was to ignore the body's needs as much as possible and eventually die to be separated from it. [12] Ever the philosopher, Socrates seemed eager to achieve this end. "Death is less terrible to…[philosophers] than to any other men," he proclaimed. [13]

The following arguments formed the backbone of the Phaedo and collectively "proved" the immortality of the soul in Socrates' mind. Opposites proved that the soul exists after the body dies, Recollection proved that the soul exists before the body is born, and Affinity proved that the soul has always existed and is therefore immortal–much like Parmenides' claim, "From nothing, nothing comes." Additionally, Socrates keeps us on the right path by sharing what the soul is *not:* a (breakable) musical instrument capable of producing harmony.

Argument 1: Opposites

Cebes answered that many feared death as the nothingness brought about by the destruction of both soul *and* body, [14] which Socrates would use as motivation to prove that the soul does not die. He first cited an "ancient tradition" that after death and residence in the Underworld, new people are born back into the world. The soul, he said, would need to exist for this to happen. [15]

Death to life meant becoming an opposite, as with life to death, [16] and both, instead of one, made more sense to Socrates than a one-way ticket to death and lack of an opposite. Without opposites, after all, the sleeping would not wake, and the awake would not sleep, [17] and therefore opposites were universal and unavoidable. If not for the life-to-death and death-to-life cycle, he insisted, where did souls come from? Souls, then, exist after death.

Argument 2: Recollection

Memory requires pre-knowledge of a given thing or concept, Socrates argued. [18] Likeness (or even unlikeness) drew connections between the thing observed and the concept behind it, [19] with the former often falling short of the latter. [20]

Socrates asked if "it is impossible to gain this knowledge, except by sight or touch or some other of the senses" [21] and was, of course, seeking a "yes." Our only path to the Forms was through observation of the physical world, however unreal the physical world was. No other forthcoming cause explained the association between specifics and their relative overarching concepts.

Filling the gap, Socrates theorized that we must have been born with pre-knowledge of the concepts, [22] identifying the loss and regaining of knowledge as "recollection." [23] As with knowledge, he declared, the soul must have been pre-existing. [24] Since Socrates has already established with opposites that the soul exists after the body, this is a second check in the immortality column.

Argument 3: Affinity

Opposites proved the soul existed after the body's death. (The path from life to death cannot exist without an accompanying death-to-life possibility.) The soul also exists before the body comes, explained via Recollection, and thus we are born already familiar with the Forms. Thus, the soul exists before and after the existence of the body.

Here Affinity comes in, sorting body and soul by what they are like to. (Merriam-Webster defines affinity as "likeness based on relationship or causal connection.") [25] Socrates used Affinity to argue for the qualities of the soul versus the physical body. He declared that "the soul is more like the invisible than the body is, and the body more like the visible." [26]

Socrates distinguished between the changing nature of concrete entities and the constant nature of their overarching concepts. [27] That which was invisible would not change, and the soul, of course, was invisible and inalterable, [28] which meant that it would not die. He did caution that the soul's integrity could be compromised, however, by caving to excessive bodily appetites (too much food, wine, sex, or feelings). [29]

Inalterability sank the final nail in. The soul could not come in or out of existence, and therefore, it must always (or never) have existed. Recollection indicates that the soul exists, otherwise we would not be able to recognize Forms, as Socrates insisted. Since the soul exists, then it must always have existed.

Harmony is not soul

Simmias raised an objection. A lyre, like the soul, could produce perfect harmony, "invisible and incorporeal," [30] but when broken, it could be played no more. This made the harmony dependent on the instrument evoking it, laying the immortal at the feet of the mortal. [31] Like the song, he concluded, humans must die never to be reborn. [32]

Another objection arose, placing Socrates' argument into doubt. [33] But he made quick work of both. He pointed out to Simmias that the invisible harmony of the lyre, unlike the incorporeal concepts they were discussing, did not exist before it was played or recollected. [34] Furthermore, the soul led the body, but the lyre's harmony was led by a visible, tangible instrument. [35] In summary, the soul was not harmony, nor harmony the soul.

In these arguments, the body and soul were separate entities and could exist independently of one another. The soul animated the body during life, uniting the parts.

Death separated them. And then life and death became a never-ending cycle as the soul waited for a new body to attach to. Two arguments showed the soul's existence before and after the body, and the third asserted its *eternal* existence.

The science on soul is fascinating, and some of it seems to point Socrates' way. "We think life is just the activity of atoms and particles which spin around for a while and then dissipate into nothingness," says a *Psychology Today* article referencing a 2011 study on quantum interference. "But if we add life to the equation, we can explain some of the major puzzles of modern science." [36]

The referenced study compared seemingly contradictory discoveries to Schrödinger's Cat, a quantum mechanics scenario devised to better understand the "wonkiness" physicists came across when investigating the world's working mechanics. Particles lacked properties until we were paying attention to them, according to Danish physicist Niels Bohr: rather than staying in a fixed position, electrons had "a 50% chance of being oriented 'up' and a 50% chance of being oriented 'down'" before observation and measurement. [37] This placed them, theoretically, in both states at once as long as no one was looking at it.

Similarly, in Schrödinger's scenario, a cat is trapped in a box containing poison with a Geiger counter and hammer pointed at some uranium. An hour elapses during which the cat may or may not die. But applying the irregularity theorized above, until the moment of observation, i.e., opening the box, scientists considered the cat both dead and alive. The implication is that when it comes to electrons and other particles, two mutually exclusive states can be understood as co-occurring: until someone or something is paying attention to it, at which point the particles will "choose" a state. This complicates our understanding of what is physically possible and occurring.

The study examined the wave nature of molecules, or atom compounds, observing the qualities of "massive tailor-made organic molecules" composed of up to 430 atoms. [38] Researchers improved on prior experiments by diffracting particles through a triple slit instead of a double one: in particular, the G1 grating (one of three) in the interferometer, used to draw information from the interference of waves, [39] "impose[d] a constraint onto the transverse molecular position that, following Heisenberg's uncertainty relation, leads to a momentum uncertainty." [40]

The data collected fit the "full quantum calculation," with researchers finding two macroscopically distinct possibilities with all atoms in the interferometer's left arm and right arm at the same time. [41] Its findings seem to confirm what Schrödinger's Cat had posited: that a theoretical cat can be both dead and alive simultaneously—and that the electrons they represented could also be positioned upward and downward or leftward and rightward, also at the same time.

Interpreting the study to mean that the things we observe only exist as such (containing "real properties") as long as we are observing them, [42] the article suggested that there is much more behind what we see and linked this back to the existence of an immortal soul. Quantum interference tends to play by its own rules, especially when beyond the scope of human perception. Kant identified our experiences as "representations," with space and time as a way to make sense of what we see rather than being objective principles of existence. [43]

In fact, the article argues, the convoluted rules of quantum mechanics are responsible for existence, meaning that the more traditional naturalistic scientific approach of life ending at death without continuance may not be right. The findings could indicate that, since it lies beyond observation, "a part of the mind–the soul–is immortal and exists outside of space and time." [44]

The study defies the commonly accepted theory of life ending at death. If an electron can indeed occupy two opposite states at the same time, and if Schrödinger's Cat can be both alive and dead simultaneously, then perhaps we do and don't die after life is complete–that is, the body dies, but the soul does not.

The legacy of Forms

Plato's Theory of Forms has dramatically impacted multiple tangents of Western philosophy, forming the foundation on which the development of metaphysics, epistemology, and ethics was built. Metaphysics is the philosophy of the nature of things, epistemology is the philosophy of knowledge, and ethics targets the rightness or wrongness of actions and thought.

Metaphysics and epistemology are closely related, with knowledge impacting what we understand about our own existence. While they examine life as it is, ethics focuses on life as it should be (the difference between normative and descriptive ethics). All three of these disciplines tie into Plato's Theory of Forms, from the appraisal of reality in the physical realm and what people can know about it, if anything, to understanding Formal perfection and following its example. Furthermore, it can all be traced back to Socrates' deathbed discussion in the "Phaedo."

The practicality of Forms extends itself to modern readers in many ways. Almost everybody understands experiences like gauging the love they share with various partners over the course of a lifetime, comparing them all against the ideal feeling, where several examples of the Form stand before the backdrop of the Form itself.

Comparisons and placing people on pedestals are generally discouraged, but you can argue through Plato that a measured dose of such activity is good for the soul. In the game of love, ideals keep standards high and foster closer matches between lovers through choosiness.

While it isn't practical to forsake the physical world entirely as Socrates was able to do, understanding our relationship through ideals gives us a greater knowledge of ourselves. And, as Plato asserted, they also help us understand the physical world: Our proximity to overarching concepts like love and courage allows us to learn what we truly need in body and soul.

Ideals also can provide a model for acting well, comparing Forms to the self instead of others, as exemplified above, which might explain why Socrates was so successful a philosopher by his own standards. Looking to ideals to adjust behavior and uplift satisfaction with life choices is a strategy that has long been in play.

But caution should be exercised when using ideals, as you'll always be coming up short. Ideals in their pure form are unachievable. You risk overwhelm, disappointment, and plain impracticality with too zealous a pursuit. Illustrating this, a 1981 summary of 91 case studies pointed out the relative weakness of the direction "do your best," finding that "cognitive behavior modification" is best achieved by setting specific goals. "No goal" and "do your best" groups underperformed but were about equal. [45] Plato's Forms fall under "do your best" because they are broad and remote. Ideals, then, may not be the best way to set goals.

However, setting specific goals *around* ideals can be a helpful workaround. By assessing desired ideals and formulating goals that will help us achieve them (or at least get closer), we are using what we can't visualize to fill in what we *can*.

This leads to knowledge acquisition regarding universal ideas, as Plato intended, and promotes self-improvement: both good goals for the philosopher in us. Despite its limitations, Plato's Theory of Forms can still aid critical thinkers today by encouraging them to take ideals into account while making goals (though ideals themselves should *not* be goals).

Action Steps

Forms and forms

This exercise will focus on identifying ideals and goals for self-improvement toward these ideals. Visual models are again featured here, requiring two lumps of modeling clay and a sheet of paper.

1. Write down one ideal you would like to work on.
2. Sculpt something that exemplifies and symbolizes that ideal, showing especially how you would like to embody this trait. (If you follow the Form of Timeliness, you might sculpt a crude watch or alarm clock.)
3. Below the ideal you desire, write down an explanation to accompany your clay sculpture as to *how* you would like to grow closer to the idea behind it.
4. Devise two S.M.A.R.T. (Specific, Measurable, Assignable, Realistic, and Time-Related) goals that will help you get there. [46]

An example of a S.M.A.R.T. goal toward Courage could involve conquering entomophobia by going to look at an insect collection two times a week. (Gradually, you would work your way up to being around *living* insects, but this is a good place to start.)

Moving On

The gap between forms and Forms is wide, and if Socrates' plea concerning wisdom is to be believed, even Plato did not have a full grasp of them. But the name of the game in philosophy is exploring the unknown, and thanks to scientific advancement, we are able to say we know much more. Yet the Forms remain intriguing and elusive.

In 399, Socrates refused to escape his fate. As he always had in life, he looked first to the form of Justice and the ethics of failing to act in accordance with it. However, doing what you *should* do can be self-defeating for people with less philosophical stamina (aka, everybody who isn't Socrates or Plato). The Swiss psychologist Jean Piaget claimed that children learn by being "little scientists as they perform experiments, make observations, and learn about the world." [47] Ideals are too distant to produce practical results here and can even end in *should* shame, so it's important to avoid discouragement and understand that not all of Plato's arguments transfer to a modern lifestyle. Ideals are best used in moderation and indirectly to help goal setting.

Chapter Summary

- The "Phaedo" depicts Socrates' last hours spent deliberating on Forms and the soul's immortality.
- Forms are invisible, eternal, and perfect, while forms are physical and changeable.
- The soul exists both prior to the body and following its death.
- Humans know the Forms prior to birth. This is how they recognize physical forms in their world.
- Invisible Forms are unchanging and thus more real than what we see. We can only know that which is always true.

5

PARMENIDES VERSUS PLATO

HOW TO PROBE THE NATURE OF REALITY, CHANGE, AND THE LIMITS OF HUMAN UNDERSTANDING

Parmenides and Zeno are infamous for terrorizing philosophers with their wacky but nigh inarguable theories regarding monism, or a perceived oneness from which all things derive. (Plato's Forms, on the other hand, fall under pluralism.) This sets up a gripping tension between student Socrates and his more experienced elders.

Zeno was Parmenides' student just as Plato was Socrates' and similarly devoted to his teacher's ideas. As Socrates put it: "Zeno here wishes to be very close to you not only in his friendship, but also in his writing." [1] He created a set of confounding paradoxes to support Parmenides' monism and belief that reality involved constant flux.

One of Zeno's paradoxes was the Arrow Paradox, which posited that because an arrow was frozen at any given moment in time, any forward or backward movement was impossible. A freeze-frame moment cannot foster movement because no time passes within it. [2] (A film reel with distinct frames is an excellent visual reference.)

The lack of movement in the arrow, in Zeno's mind, proved monism true. In isolating movement, he highlighted the singular moment and presented it as one. And just as Socrates would run into trouble against Parmenidean Monism in Plato's "Parmenides," so, too, do many of us.

Zeno's Arrow Paradox shows the divide between One and many, how an arrow's movement can be seen as occupying a single place instead of many others. As will be seen in this chapter, Parmenides used his idea of the One to point out the contradictions in Plato's pluralistic Theory of Forms.

Brace yourself for the essential concepts of the "Parmenides," Plato's most difficult dialogue. Though difficult to understand, these points will tie together later. (Contradiction is the main theme here.) The work highlights Socrates' trademark dialectic: asking question after question until a concluding theory or compromising difficulty is reached. Through complex arguments, Plato (and Socrates) targeted the nature of reality from a variety of angles.

Difficulties for Plato

In the "Parmenides," Plato places the plurality of Forms under fire in a discussion that probably never happened historically. [3] Its thoroughness as a counterargument to one of his most famous theories nonetheless makes it an integral stop on our journey. The dialogue also features a teenage Socrates acting as student to Zeno and Parmenides and letting them lead the discussion.

Through Plato, Zeno and Parmenides provide compelling and sophisticated counterarguments that, if indeed invented, show Plato's thoroughness in regard to his own ideas. He depicted Socrates as a man who would not stop asking probing questions, even if it ended in his death. This devotion to sound theory and right knowledge may partially explain why Plato's works, in general, have aged so well.

In this dialogue, Plato built on the connection between reality and Forms, as well as the relationship between Forms and their manifestations in the physical world. Questions such as, "Can a form partake in a Form without *being* a Form?" and "Is a Form One or many?" are asked and answered. One objection, in particular, proves strong against Plato's Forms: the Third Man Argument, which will be covered later in the chapter.

Plato subjected his arguments to two of the era's best (and most radical) critical thinkers, drawing from their insights to fortify his own. Zeno and Parmenides first appeared to reject Socrates' theories regarding Form. Later in the dialogue, however, Parmenides seemed to be at least partially on board, claiming that Socrates was merely too inexperienced to conquer the difficulties laid out by his elder philosophers. [4]

Parmenides hailed from Elea and was known for his radical yet difficult-to-disprove ideas. Plato aged him at about 65 years in 450 B.C.E. when the discussion occurred. Zeno, also from Elea, would have been about 40. [5] The dialogue begins with the transferal of Zeno's writings from Athens to Cerameicus, where the dialogue takes place. [6]

Plato would not be born for another 20 years, and it appears that he himself devised the conversation as a response to his "Theory of Forms." [7] In reversing Socrates' role from teacher to student as a literary device, he heightened the gap between Socrates' philosophical identity as a young man and an old one. Plato himself was a teacher, and this literary device gave him a chance to figuratively mold the mind of his greatest influencer.

The "Parmenides" is split into two parts: the discussion with Socrates and the discussion with Aristoteles (not Aristotle). The first half begins with Socrates reading Zeno's treatises and asking about them. Afterward, Zeno and Parmenides lead the conversation with Socrates interjecting as a student, following Plato's (and Socrates') dialogue-based model. Recall that Plato depicted Socrates dying shortly after introducing the Forms in the "Phaedo," so it's likely that the more sophisticated assertions expressed here were more Plato's because he had the time to develop them.

With several arguments and one "great difficulty," [8] the first part of the dialogue seemingly spells doom for the Forms. Surprisingly (or perhaps not so surprisingly due to his age), Socrates could not defend the Theory of Forms. In his callow youth, he made the mistake of agreeing too quickly with the Eleatics, and his portion ended in puzzlement as in Plato's early dialogues. From there, Parmenides and Zeno took up the slack with Aristotles.

Plato placed this faltering early on and presented the moment of puzzlement in the middle instead of at the end. This shift shows the complexity of his middle works that had developed from shorter early works.

Although Socrates could not win the argument, Plato probably could have. Instead, he allowed the character of young Socrates to fumble, revealing the difficulties to a less-honed mind, and egged on similarly-inexperienced readers to fumble with him, learning things for themselves.

Though impressed by his natural talent for philosophy, Parmenides kindly told Socrates that he tried "too soon, before […] properly trained, to define the beautiful, the just, the good, and all the other ideas." [9]. He urged Socrates to develop his natural abilities and directed him to Zeno for training. [10] He also cautioned Socrates to consider what would occur if his hypothesis was false. [11]

The second part of the dialogue continues to confound scholars, and a multitude of different interpretations lie behind it. There are eight deductions and an appendix in all, covering the nuance of parts within wholes, whether or not the One "is," and whether others can exist outside the One. The first two deductions and appendix especially created further difficulties for Plato and Socrates.

Socrates' take: An initial blow to Forms

Parmenides and Zeno exposed inconsistencies regarding the Theory of Forms, beginning with the tension between One and many. (Since the conversation was probably made up later, Plato would have had ample time to make this consideration before writing about it here.)

Zeno shot down pluralism with the following argument: "if existences are many, they must be both like and unalike, which is impossible; for the unalike cannot be like, nor the like unalike." [12] But Socrates pointed out that things can be like in some ways and unalike in others, simultaneously One and many, when Form is distinguished from forms. [13]

For example, Socrates is like the Form of Man in resemblance but unlike him in being just one in a group of humans, and he is also one man composed of multiple parts. Likewise, "rest and motion" could coexist side-by-side [14] when moving a part of your body while the rest of you remains still.

The discussion built in complexity from there. The singular ideated identity of "the One" [15] could not occur in many distinct bodies away from itself as with a Form and forms, according to Parmenides. That would make it "separate from itself," an impossibility.

Socrates argued that a Form "might be like day," singular in existence but occurring in many different places. [16] However, Parmenides quickly shot this down by citing a large sail covering multiple people, forcing Socrates to admit that parts of the sail covered several individuals. [17] Hence, various parts of day hit distinct areas of the world. Daylight would also feature symbolically in another of Plato's middle works, "The Republic," in the "Allegory of the Cave" and the "Allegory of the Sun."

The Third Man Argument, so named for the requirement of a third unifying party over Forms and forms, followed, tackling Socrates' claim that the same idea occurs in forms, and between forms and the Form. He believed that this sameness made the Form One in each distinct instance rather than many (a Form of Love, a Form of Courage, etc.), [18] a confusing detail in Plato's pluralistic approach. (Both he and Socrates still appeared to consider the Forms all together as many, not one.) In response, Parmenides remarked on the relation between Form and form. Multiple forms were linked by their likeness into a group (f). [19]

Furthermore, because these forms were similar to the Form, they were linked by association. This created a group of forms and Form sharing likeness. ([f + F]). [20] But this group would necessitate another Form–the Third Man–over it to connect all the like items [(f + F] + F1). The combination of form, Form, and uber-Form, in turn, needed yet another Form over *that* to group the like items, and so on. [21] Therefore, the Form could not be One.

In addition, Forms cannot be considered distinct from the physical realm according to the "great difficulty" described by Parmenides. He exemplified this through the relationships between Master and Slave and master and slave, showing that Forms (abstract) and forms (physical) do not interact. Tweaking master and slave to teacher and student, the physical teacher shares a relationship with the physical student but not with the Forms Plato associates with them (Teacher and Student): the Form of Teacher has no relation to the particular student, and likewise for the Form of Student and particular teacher. [22] Because the abstract and physical don't interact, Parmenides concluded that as physical beings, our knowledge is limited to the physical world. This means we can't have knowledge of the Forms. [23]

These inconsistencies and the disconnect between Forms and the physical world seemed to seal the fate of Plato's "Theory of Forms." But a clever twist on the Eleatics' part may have shown that all was not lost. The many different interpretations of the following section do not stem from a lack of clarity. They are merely so intricate and abstract that they can be taken in many ways.

<u>Aristoteles' take: Further difficulties related to the One</u>

When Aristoteles took Socrates' place as the student, the dialogue turned in a yet more winding direction. Two Deductions and an Appendix delve into the Being of the One and whether or not it is continuous, exposing various contradictions. These arguments are more fleshed out than the ones in the previous section but possibly even more inscrutable. Six more deductions follow outlining various ramifications, but we'll reserve focus for the first two.

While Plato provided the dialectical framework and Theory of Forms, Parmenides' influence is clear in the intricate and esoteric direction the dialogue takes. These concepts come to the forefront in the following two deductions and appendix: part, whole, many, One, and Being.

The First Deduction

Parmenides indicated that the One is neither comprised of parts nor whole. It is not parts because then the One would be multiple: a contradiction. It is not whole because wholes encompass many parts. [24] It cannot be temporal (subject to time and aging/further development) because beginning, middle, and end are all parts it cannot contain. Thus, it is eternal and unchanging. [25] It also lacks a physical form, being neither round nor built of straight lines. [26]

Nor can the One be "either in anything else or in itself." [27] It has no parts, therefore cannot be in anything else. It cannot be inside itself because that would mean being at least two parts, one of which exists within the other. [28] Because the One is neither in itself nor anything else, it seems it must be whole. And yet it is not, because to be whole is to be composed of parts.

Similarly, the One is unchanging, and because it cannot change, it also cannot move. But because it is never in anything (see paragraph above), it is "never in the same," meaning that it could not be at rest *or* in motion. [29] Both are a continuous state of sameness, which is not to say that something in motion is never at rest. However, *while* something is in a state of motion, it is never at rest, and vice versa.

The "Parmenides" is known for these head-exploding contradictions. Determining any type of continuity is nigh impossible, and the Second Deduction is a little better than the First.

<u>The Second Deduction</u>

Both this Deduction and the following Appendix (see below) concern the Being of the One. Beginning with if One *is*, Parmenides argues under the assumption that One "partakes of Being" and Being is, therefore, a quality found in the One. [30] By virtue of being part of Being, the One comprises at least two parts, as Being and One are considered separately. [31]

The separation between the One and Being means that the One has parts. Having parts implies it has a beginning, middle, and end. The beginning comes before the other parts and the end after. These other parts are portions of both the One and the whole (comprising the One and the other parts). [32]

The parts and the One together only become complete when the end comes, [33] indicating that the One could not have come before or after the others and must be the same age. [34] This, of course, is a strike against the One as atemporal and eternal.

The One is accused of being both temporal and atemporal, confined and limitless. The truth must lie somewhere in between.

Appendix to the First and Second Deductions

Exploiting the contradictions he found, Parmenides then flipped the coin on the first two Deductions to question whether there were times the One *didn't* take part in Being. [35] The only way for the One to take part, yet not take part, in Being is if it were partaking or not at different times from one another. [36] This must mean it underwent a change to get to the other state. [37]

Briefly reassuming that the One is: If it changes (as it must, understood to be both changing and unchanging) and if it *is*, then this means it must have experienced an *isn't* at some point. [38] The Deduction following the Appendix extrapolates this principle to other opposing qualities such as "separate and combined" and "like and unalike," noting that they were at times one and at other times another. [39]

The Third Man argument concluded that we cannot know the Forms. A barrier between the Forms and the physical world was thus exposed, limiting our knowledge to worldly concerns.

What does this mean for reality?

Before, in the "Phaedo," Plato claimed that we could not know anything changeable, so we could not know the physical realm. Yet Parmenides seems to indicate here that that's all we *can* know. At such an impasse, what are we to do?

Our closer proximity to the physical realm makes it a more intuitive choice. But perhaps it is better to lean into the contradictions that Parmenides laid out, conceding that just as the physical realm is knowable in some ways and unknowable in others, the Forms may also be simultaneously knowable and unknowable.

This sets up a complexity to Beingness and knowledge both. It becomes difficult to ascertain, within this complexity, what is and isn't possible or knowable; thus, a dose of humility is important in navigating the questions that arise.

For Parmenides, change was an inevitable part of existence, which tends to make more sense to us than the abstraction of Forms. His insights are useful not just in navigating change but encouraging sensory interaction with your surroundings. Anticipating and embracing change and fully partaking in Being will help you greatly in life, and you can put these ideas into practice by learning everything you can about your own life to try and track when it might alter in the future. Getting a savings account is a Parmenides-approved activity for keeping abreast of change and the existence of "rainy days."

A 2022 review in *Nature Reviews Psychology* assessed intellectual humility as "recognizing that there are gaps in one's knowledge and that one's current beliefs might be incorrect." [40] A 2020 study covered in this review showed that adopting such humility and listening to other points of view usually means attaining greater life satisfaction. A survey among wisdom researchers found that 80% associated wisdom with an "orientation towards shared humanity." ("Pursuit of truth" came second at 69%.) [41]

But knowing you have a knowledge gap can be a bit of a catch-22. Thankfully, a 2015 analysis of 40 literature reviews gives us a roadmap for pinpointing knowledge gap in a research context (research gap). Three different types of coding were used to sort the data: elaborative ("'analyzing textual data in order to develop theory further'"), open ("'generating higher-abstraction level type categories from sets of concepts/variables'"), and axial ("'relating concepts/categories to each other'"). [42] These revealed 555 research gaps across the forty papers.

Identifying research gaps is a four-part process, the study found: localization, characterization, verification, and presentation. Localization is identification on a smaller scale, involving "gaps that require further research" before they can be identified. [43] Characterization organizes research gaps by why they exist, verification confirms that the gap *does* exist, and presentation means sharing the gap in literary reviews.

We can use this guidance on research gaps to try to recognize knowledge gaps in ourselves. It begins with a suspicion: something that needs further research, as the "localization" step confirms. You probably don't need to worry about characterization outside of research purposes, but it may help you better understand knowledge gaps to come. Verify the gap through research, and if you want to help others overcome this knowledge gap, too, then by all means, share with the class.

Although knowledge gaps are no doubt a humbling experience, humility can be a touchy subject when it comes to what we know. We as a species tend to like patting ourselves on the back, *especially* about what we know (believing that our rational capabilities set us apart). It's an ongoing process, but you can speed it up by catching errors as they occur and being honest with yourself about what you know versus what you *think* you know.

The latter is no easy task, especially when a defensive attitude can enter the equation. Discerning opinion from fact is something we all think we've mastered, but almost everybody ends up believing in some falsehood. Think about the "fact" presented in Chapter 4 that the sky is blue. Many accept this statement, even though it isn't always true. The minute size of the technicality is a bit unforgiving, but you have to train yourself to make these distinctions in order to pick up on knowledge gaps. Epistemological humility speeds up the process by disallowing complacency and letting knowledge gaps slide.

Understanding wisdom as being in tune with others (and the world) opens the possibility of knowledge back up. The sharing of different perspectives means that people have access to knowledge they would otherwise lack. Paying attention to the physical realm is the best path to knowledge acquisition.

Action Steps

Ramifications of Change

Parmenides believed that change was always on the horizon, and this exercise will help you anticipate and mentally prepare for this change.

1. Grab a tape recorder or a recording app on your phone. Turn it on and name the next big change you are preparing to undergo (a promotion, a move, etc.) If there isn't one, predict one or make an educated guess.
2. Discuss how this change will affect you, what you have done to prepare, and what you need to do to prepare.
3. Discuss how this change will affect others, separating them one by one to ensure direct empathy with individuals rather than groups. Don't brush off this consideration, even if it seems like you are the only one affected. Chances

are that others will be, as well. If you truly don't know, then hypothesize as before.
4. Did any new insights or feelings arise from Step 3? Did it change how you see the change or how you are going to prepare? With this in mind, go back and repeat Step 2.

Moving On

Humility and thinking of others lead to wisdom. Building knowledge based on the world around us is all we have, if Parmenides is to be believed and, thus, it's important to take full advantage of this approach.

The "Parmenides" is a difficult dialogue, and its ideas can be interpreted in many ways. If we can take away anything from reading it, it's that the physical realm is much more important than Plato gives it credit for. Taking this forward into the "Cave Allegory", it becomes evident that interpretation is just as important as the text itself.

Chapter Summary

- Zeno's Arrow Paradox engendered his and Parmenides' belief in the One over Plato's many Forms.
- In the "Parmenides," a teenage Socrates argued for the existence of Forms.

- Parmenides' Third Man argument showed an infinite loop created by grouping a Form with its particulars, necessitating a Form over it to unite the parts.
- Parmenides pointed out a "great difficulty–" that physical beings can only know the physical realm.
- In the Aristoteles section, contradictions abound, including the claim that the One is both limited and limitless.
- As Socrates showed, humility in knowledge acquisition is essential.

6

PLATO'S FAMOUS CAVE ALLEGORY

HOW TO STEP INTO THE LIGHT AND WALK TOWARD THE TRUTH IN YOUR EVERYDAY LIFE

Next time you watch a movie, turn down the volume so that you can't understand the dialogue and close your eyes. You should still be able to see bright colors inside your eyelids. Your ears will pick up on the movie sounds without quite being able to make sense of them.

Keep your eyes closed long enough to become accustomed to the dulled sensory experience. Then open them, turn the volume back up, and think about how much more you understand from the movie. This is a basic idea of Plato's "Allegory of the Cave" from "The Republic."

The abstraction of the "Cave Allegory" means that, like the "Parmenides," it is interpreted in different ways. However, it is much easier to read and understand on a basic level. In fact, Plato's "Cave Allegory" is one of his most renowned ideas and, as noted earlier, has turned up just about everywhere, even outside philosophy.

Diving into the meaning of the allegory, one clear point Plato made was that looking beyond the physical promoted critical thinking. This lends itself nicely to everyday life, as when considering signs of the ideal job in your current job. Whatever your specific needs, the "Allegory of the Cave" quite likely fits into them.

Unpacking Plato's Allegory of the Cave

The "Cave Allegory" depicted a group of people in a cave, chained to the wall, stuck gazing at shadows. The cave allowed light, Plato said, and the cave dwellers were "able to look forward only," unable to see one another. [1] A fire burned between the cave entrance and the cave dwellers, which allowed them to see shadows of people and objects on the wall in front of them. This meant that the shadows on the wall were their reality, and nothing existed outside of them in their minds. [2]

When one of the cave dwellers was "freed from his fetters" and able to leave the cave, the sun temporarily blinded him. [3] Because the allegory concerned education and lack thereof, Plato painted the cave dwellers' exit from the cave and journey into the light as analogous to philosophers discovering the Forms. [4] A strong literary symbolism courses through this portion of the "Republic," adding to its lasting appeal.

One of the most famous philosophical passages in Western thought, the "Cave Allegory" inspired renowned literary works and a quarrel between Martin Heidegger and Hannah Arendt. In the 17th century, philosopher and politician Francis Bacon borrowed the idea for his *idola specus* ("Idols of the Cave") logical fallacy concept of biases creating "errors of reason." [5]

Many other inspirations and dialogues followed this, debating the allegory's true meaning. Leaving the cave can denote accessing a higher level of knowledge regarding why (and how) things are the way they are, as Plato argued. It can also be applied to just about any change that leads to increased life satisfaction: Adequately caring for yourself takes a type of knowledge, and the better you get at it, the happier you are.

Learning has other upsides, as well. A 1962 preschool intervention program followed up with participants 37 years later to assess how lasting initial benefits, related to social and economic improvements, were. In 1962, the Perry Preschool Program (PPP) randomly assigned 123 preschool children to either an education or control group, with the education group offering "a 2-year program of 2.5 hours of interactive academic instruction daily coupled with 1.5-hour weekly home visits." [6]

Intervention participants finished more schooling, made more money, and had more stable families when they were reinterviewed at 40 although they oddly reported more medical conditions than the control group despite having better health status and insurance. This meant health benefits were limited but did not cancel out the socioeconomic benefits discovered.

The intervention's findings confirm what Plato knew: that education uplifts us. In the "Cave Allegory," Plato theorized about knowledge and reality regarding the Forms and how they connect with human nature. The Forms are real and unchanging, he argued, and because they are unchanging, they are all we can truly know. Although Plato's Forms took a beating in the last chapter, they are presented here with confidence. The physical realm, again, is downplayed.

Plato's cave dwellers represented humans before they were educated, with their perception limited in imprisonment. The fire in the cave only created enough light to make shadows, so they could barely see, and they were unable to even interact with one another because they could only stare forward at the shadows. [7] Their chains made it impossible to remove themselves. But since this is all they thought reality was, they may not have even felt the urge.

The cave dwellers' reality was a mere fraction of the actual reality from which they had been taken, presumably at birth. In real life, Plato asserted, people were analogous to the cave dwellers in their lack of curiosity beyond sensory details. Living only in the physical world and reacting only to physical stimuli wasted the mind but especially the soul, which could be damaged by "food and similar pleasures and gluttonies." [8] His solution was for people to metaphorically exit the cave and look to the Forms for further knowledge.

Leaving the cave

"An eye [...] could not be converted to the light from the darkness except by turning the whole body," Plato said, [9] highlighting the commitment and thoroughness it took to alter towards enlightenment. "Turning the whole body" meant shifting focus from particulars to Forms. This action resulted in "becoming together with the entire soul" until the soul could see past the dazzling blindness of the Forms. [10]

When the imprisoned cave dwellers escaped and overcame their blindness under sudden sunlight, they were being enlightened. Their interactions with real things in place of shadows marked the beginning of the human journey of recognizing things larger than the self. For the first time, they were experiencing the world as it truly is.

This placed focus back on education. At the end of the "Cave Allegory," Plato declared that the wisest people had a duty to return to the cave and inform the cave dwellers:

If you had a better education, you were "more capable of sharing both ways of life," Plato proclaimed. Thus, "down you must go [...] to the habitation of the others and accustom yourselves to the observation of the obscure things there." [11]

This idea was unpopular with Plato's brother Glaucon, a speaker in the "Republic." Glaucon accused Socrates of condemning these enlightened former prisoners who had left the cave to an "inferior life." [12] Nevertheless, Plato believed that the risks should not hold people back from uplifting others who need it.

Plato's emphasis on society is important in dissecting the "Cave Allegory" and his intention behind it. Beyond the "Cave Allegory," the "Republic" extrapolates the reward of a well-regulated soul to that of a well-regulated society. Personal betterment is only half of the journey he intended for us. The other half entails going out and engaging people in a dialogue, as Socrates did for as long as he could.

Giving back to society through dialogue is about finding balance, as is deciding when to focus on remote ideals and when to zero in on the physical world. Poem upon poem will tell you to stop and smell the roses, and as Plato himself noted, living bodies have real appetites to temper that anchor them physically. Striking balance between that and the abstract is essential.

The Forms, eternal essences in the physical world, play an important role in the "Allegory of the Cave." They are represented by everything we can see under the sunlight. As for everything that we *actually* see under the sunlight: the Forms lie yet beyond them, casting shadows on the cave walls. (Yet the shadows are likenesses, not Forms themselves.)

This is a bit of a difficulty, given Parmenides' more intuitive stance that the physical world is all we *can* know. Whether or not you feel you need to focus on the abstract is up to you and your sensibilities.

The answer, again, usually lies somewhere in the middle: even the most tactile person can find value in ideals, like satin with an unattainably perfect weave. In modest doses, ideals both soothe us regarding the world's imperfections, which we can't control, and inspire us to improve ourselves, which we *can*. But anybody who loves tangling with the big questions and perfect-yet-remote ideals needs to ground themselves in the real world every once in a while. Ideals can be addictive, but as Socrates pointed out, the body still needs caring for! Balance between the physical world and the realm of fancy is essential.

<u>Plato's cave in the everyday</u>

Discovering and accepting the Forms may take you out of whatever metaphorical cave you find yourself trapped in. If you're the type who finds it difficult to speak up at work, then maybe the inner peace you find after doing so is your version of leaving the cave. Nerves can make it a messy process, sometimes resulting in word salad and second-guessing what you said. But practice makes perfect, and confidence eventually follows, as does the relative ease of repeating an action you've just completed for the first time.

When the metaphor is extended to other circumstances, there can be many things keeping you in your cave: fear that life won't change after trying something new, feeling too tired after dealing with everyday struggles, attachment to current habits, and the like. One of the most common barriers is self-doubt.

Think about the hurdles you face in improving your life satisfaction. Think about what might be keeping you from clearing them or even tackling them at all. What, if anything, is overwhelming you currently? If surrounded by a messy home, cleaning up an area of it will get you that much closer to realizing the feeling of being in a clean environment. (It also requires the knowledge of cleaning.)

Perhaps the barrier is people-related. If people walk all over your boundaries because you don't enforce them, then speaking up will give you the experience of what it feels like to be heard and respected. Building interpersonal skills is a way of working to better understand the world around you.

Whatever your aim, make sure you are gaining more knowledge instead of becoming set in your ways. Leaving the cave is about learning above all, and changing your personal circumstances should lead to satisfaction and a wiser perspective. The first step is usually the hardest: identifying the shackles that hold you back.

A 2015 article on habit-forming defined habits as "learned automatic responses with specific features." [13] Though tough to break, they can be replaced by healthier habits, especially when paired with goals. The idea is that it gets easier each time you do it, to the point where it becomes ingrained.

A 2016 set of two studies found that creating new habits made it so "behavior change interventions can be designed to habitize a new behavior so that it is maintained despite short-term desires and temptations."[14] The first experiment encouraged participants with bad eating habits to eat chocolate, which they not only did, but lost some self-control in doing so. The second study built on this by offering carrots to people with *healthy* habits and then later presenting them with M&Ms. But the participants still chose carrots as long as the "habit cue," i.e., a picture of carrots, was there. Those who had healthier habits successfully resisted temptation, indicating that when a good habit is established, it holds strong.

Habit formation is a powerful tactic, especially when combined with the knowledge acquisition that comes from exploring the world and your connection with it. Getting yourself out of the cave might just be a matter of making a single change and sticking with it. As with vision adjusting to outside light in the allegory, the adjustment period is the most difficult part.

Action Steps

Leaving The Cave: A Way For Each Weekday

1. *Keep a journal.* Write about life events, but also examine the everyday minutiae as Socrates did. In doing so, you may discover new insights regarding things you never really thought about before.
2. *Watch a documentary.* One of the easiest ways to get out of your comfort zone and learn something new is by watching an educational film. Bonus points if you can watch it in a theater, which provides more sensory ambience.
3. *Join a class.* If you want to get out and socialize while you learn, then this is a good option. You might also benefit from other people's knowledge while you are adding to your own, which means faster learning.
4. *Visit a library.* Introverts may prefer a trip to the library, where people are around but they aren't expected to interact. Self-study means learning at your own pace, or as fast as you can read. You also have access to a greater knowledge base here.
5. *Go on a walk.* You'd be surprised at what you can learn just by taking a quick trip outdoors and observing more than you normally do. Whether watching people or animals, leaves or sidewalks,

there is always something new to see.
Interpretation is just as important as the text itself.

Moving On

Plato's "Cave Allegory" had a profound impact on society, inspiring countless literary works and even films like *The Matrix* and *Rebel Without A Cause* (which featured a character named Plato). [15] It has spurred Bacon, Heidegger, and other philosophers to chime in with their own commentary. Whatever the medium, the theme of reality not being what we think is evidently too enticing to ignore.

Chapter Summary

- In the "Republic's" "Allegory of the Cave," imprisoned people watch shadows on the walls cast by real items outside but believe the shadows to be their reality.
- In a pre-educated state, people are like cave dwellers. When they educate themselves, they become unchained and able to leave the cave.
- The sun illuminates the objects that cast shadows, and by seeing these real things, the liberated cave dwellers see that the cave setting is not reality.

- We are the cave dwellers, Plato analogized, and Forms are the real things outside, visible only to those who could reason.
- According to Plato, reasoning about the true reality (Forms) eventually leads to minimization of physical needs while knowledge and life satisfaction are gained.

7
BASK IN THE PHILOSOPHER KING'S GLORY
WHAT DOES IT TAKE TO BECOME A WISE SUCCESSFUL LEADER

Think about the last ruler you have come across who remained uncorrupted by power. They're rather rare. As historian Lord Acton declared: "Power tends to corrupt. Absolute power corrupts absolutely." [1]

That being said, research highlights a complicated relationship between power and corruption. Rather than power inevitably leading to corruption, a ruler's "corruption" seemed to come from predetermined factors, one study argued.

A 2012 experiment involving 173 adults found that those with a lower moral identity exhibited higher self-interested behaviors. [2] Moral identity (MI) refers to how important empathy is to a person. Researchers split the experiment into two phases, a survey followed by the experiment, occurring a week apart. [3]

Using Aquino and Reed's five-item scale to ascertain how much "a person's moral identity is core to his or her sense of self" in the first phase, researchers measured participants' MI [4]. They then assigned an essay detailing an ordinary day to some participants. They told others to write about a time in which they felt they had power, following up with a "dictator game" assessing self-interest. [5]

During the game, participants were paired and informed of an impending lottery for a "$100 gift certificate for an online retailer," for which they would earn tickets based on their and their partner's performance. [6] 10 points were available to choose from, and leftover points went to the partner. Taking more points meant better chances–unless they took too many and the lottery was canceled. [7] On the whole, the participants claimed an average of 5.41 points for themselves. [8] but the participants tasked with writing about a time when they felt powerful created an MI-based split in the results: low MI participants kept about 7.5 points, and high MI participants around 5.5. [9] This showed a "significant interaction between manipulated power and moral identity." [10]

Power can bring out nasty traits in a person with low MI, but not a person who maintains empathy and moral sensitivity even as their power grows. In fact, high MI people were actually *more* generous when reminded of community, not less. As Plato's philosopher king encouraged, living moderately could be the answer. Following the model of the "Republic" means increasing moral identity and maintaining it at a high level. This type of person might have what it takes to be a good leader.

Plato's ideal society, and his philosopher king within it, continues to intrigue readers. Some still tout the benefits of a three-class system (ruling class, military, and producers–farmers, laborers, professionals, etc.) aligning with the three parts of the soul, although some weaknesses are also evident. Still, we can take pieces of his idyllic society and try to apply them to our own.

Presenting the philosopher king

In the "Republic," Socrates proclaimed that unless philosophers become kings or kings become philosophers, "there can be no cessation of troubles, dear Glaucon, for our states, nor, I fancy, for the human race either." [11] He lacked confidence that humans could successfully regulate their souls unless they had been trained in doing so. This meant training in philosophy.

The philosopher king played an important role in leading the city with their wisdom. To keep everyone in line and the philosopher king in power, Socrates suggested a "Noble Lie." Everyone had a type of metal intermingled in their person: guardians (rulers) were gold, the military class silver, and the producers iron and brass. [12] We'll examine the ramifications of this ordering later on in the chapter.

These three classes comprised the ideal society and corresponded with the cardinal virtues: courage, temperance, wisdom, and justice (which required the other three. The military class must have courage, [13] the producers temperance, [14] and the guardian class wisdom. The guardian class was designated the smallest class. [15]

Within the guardian class, the philosopher king rules Plato's hypothetical city, just as wisdom is meant to rule the soul. Stripping the city of distractions, he argued, ensured that each class would fulfill its function and create a balanced social environment. [16] He also endorsed abolishing most private property and distributing wealth and possession more equally, living with each other in "a common mess like soldiers on campaign." [17]

Socrates acknowledged that this might not make individuals happy. Rather, his aim was the happiness of the whole, which he achieved with the harmonious city that had arisen in dialogue.

Adeimantus, another brother of Plato present in the dialogue, objected that most known philosophers who had received the training Socrates described were unscrupulous and, therefore, useless to the state. [18] This denotes potential philosopher kings who are truly ready for kinship as rare.

Indeed, this rarity indicates that Plato is asking a lot of us, even by a philosopher's standards. Very few people at the time or now would hit all the criteria. It begs the question: Does the paragon philosopher king really exist at all?

As it turns out, not all of Plato's ideas translate to modern society. In James Surowiecki's *Wisdom of Crowds*, the eponymous concept indicates that groups come up with wiser decisions than people, seemingly dooming the all-wise philosopher king to nonexistence. [19] Free-market economics operates on this concept, in which prices are determined by a guiding "invisible hand" - or the self-interested actions of buyers and sellers. The theory posits that self-interest by this group creates societal benefit. [20] Thus, the wisdom of the group outpaces the wisdom of the philosopher king.

But if Plato is right about philosophical education helping regulate the soul to bring lasting contentment, such training is still worth pursuing. After all, it makes sense that a soul without conflict means a happier life. The concept of philosopher kingship can benefit anyone, not just those focusing on leadership positions.

<u>Distinguishing factors of philosopher kings</u>

Every cardinal virtue shown by the other classes had to exist in the philosopher king at an appropriate level. The most important of these was wisdom. Courage and temperance followed, bringing about an excellence of soul (aka, justice).

Socrates distinguished true philosophers from the "lovers of spectacle and the arts," [21] or people who would publicly argue for praise. "Those for whom the truth is the spectacle of which they are enamored," [22] he insisted, were the truer philosophers.

Philosophers had to love the truth, not just commit to telling it. This naturally correlated with wisdom. [23] Philosophers also followed the true path of accruing wisdom, thus regulating the soul and lessening inclinations of the body that hindered the soul. Additionally, the true philosopher was unswayed by material rewards and kept an open mind. [24] Yet today, we see that no one exists completely without inclinations. This comprises part of the impracticality of the philosopher king.

Plato summed up the true philosopher as a man of "good memory, quick apprehension, magnificent, gracious, friendly, and akin to truth, justice, bravery, and sobriety." [25] Wisdom (affinity with truth), courage, and temperance were prerequisites for the soul to excel and be understood as just, which will be further explored in Chapter 8.

These qualities worked well for kingship. To expand the philosopher pool, Plato even asserted that women had the same potential and should be given the same education as men, along with the ability to become a philosopher king. [26] Some of these elements, such as the analogy between soul and city and the importance of leading courage and temperance with reason, still appeal to many.

Educating future rulers

Preparing someone for rule is no easy task, especially if you plan for them to develop the right temperament that will not be corrupted. Plato devoted a good portion of text to this very topic and related discussions, exploring how the philosopher king's education would differ from the two other classes.

Socrates suggested gymnastics for the body and music for the soul, along with telling philosopher kings in training fables as a moral teaching aid so they could better understand facts later. [27] He advised censoring the poets (including Homer), claiming they "composed false stories which they told and still tell to mankind." [28] The distinction between these "false stories" and fables is thin, and Homer and Hesiod can be understood as didactic, as well. Plato's distaste for the poets therefore doesn't hold much water with modern readers anymore, especially those who enjoy a wider berth of ancient Greek literature than Plato alone.

Future philosopher kings also had to show valor, being "more afraid of slavery than of death." [29] They could not be too sensitive and were disallowed from lamentation. [30] This seems to recall the scene in the "Phaedo," in which Socrates chastises his friends for weeping over him. As the first of Plato's middle works, the "Phaedo" would have been written before the "Republic" but in the same general era.

Truth was important above all. Lying was considered "as subversive and destructive of a state as it is of a ship." [31] In desiring opposite traits, Plato (and Socrates) also disallowed tales of intemperance, folly, and cowardice. [32] By providing future rulers with a round education, they'd be trained to be inquisitive, open-minded, and always searching for the truth.

Education was integral to philosopher kings, molding not just their knowledge but their disposition as well. Being a good ruler meant having to prepare extensively for a variety of situations but also be able to improvise. Having the right mindset around rule could mean the difference between success and failure.

Adopting the philosopher king model

A good leader is hard to find, but not impossible. If we start educating our future leaders as Plato suggested, they may excel yet higher. He spoke of early education, but education can start at any age. Duly prepared for office, the future philosopher king will be more comfortable and confident and likely rule more wisely.

Having a capable ruler makes for a more harmonious society. Think of the times when you feel best about your life. Chances are, they occurred when you felt more balanced and in control. It can be useful to imagine yourself as philosopher king, benevolently ruling over the various aspects of your life with wisdom. How have you created a more harmonious life for yourself?

Being philosopher king means making sure that your city is in good order, especially the military and producer classes. If unhappy, either one could start a disruptive rebellion, much like how appetitive or emotional parts in an individual soul can act up and overtake reason resulting in poor impulse control and querulousness. Above all, you must look to the whole for confirmation that everything is indeed functioning properly.

When extrapolating the city to the soul as Plato did, being philosopher king means upholding the virtues of temperance, courage, and wisdom and leading with the latter. This makes sense; ensuring you don't drink too much at a party and forcing yourself to deal with stressful situations are generally good actions to live by. Ruling a city also meant staying in your lane–focusing on wisdom– and not interfering with duties of the military class and producers. [33] Like a single banana that opens to three peels, an individual's outer maintenance (performing sole assigned cardinal virtue) differed from their inner maintenance (performing all three cardinal virtues).

Do you make decisions based on reason or on intuition? Both are powerful motivators, although Plato prefers reason. One of a set of 4 experiments in 1975 presented participants with equally valuable gift packages containing cash and coupons and tasked them with filling in a missing value based on the values of the other components. [34] (Gift package A contained coupons worth $32 plus an undetermined amount of cash, while Gift package B had $20 in cash and $18 in coupons. Participants had to fill in a cash value for Gift package A based on the aggregate value of Gift package B and what they thought it was worth.) [35]

A week after this task, researchers asked participants to choose between them and also tell the researchers whether cash or coupons were more important to them. 88% percent chose whichever was more important to them, indicating some sort of rationale even when both choices were touted as equal. Shafir et al. concluded that "people seem to be following a choice mechanism that is easy to explain and justify: choosing according to the more important dimension provides a better reason for choice than, say, random selection." [36]

But "reason" in this sense relies on what we *think* is true. Here "reason" means "rationale" and leaves room for subjectivity, whereas the type of reason claimed to result in better decisions is a more objective kind limited to *sound* reason. And we don't always know when our beliefs are false or misguided, complicating matters. Thus, reason alone might not be the way to go, although you can still work on developing your ability to use it. Incorporating intuition and the emotion behind it in your decision-making is a better choice.

Both intuition and sound reasoning make good skills in a leader. Optimistically, research implies that just about anyone is capable of leadership. A 2008 review of studies on "heritability and human development" found that genetics play a smaller role in leadership development than experience, which amounts to about 70%. [37] This supports Plato's insistence on heavily educating the philosopher kings.

In a 2014 study, 165 students taking a leadership theory course were surveyed before and after the course's duration. The "unique, 66-item" survey combined three well-known leadership scales to assess whether students were ready, willing, and able to fulfill leadership positions and was conducted before and after the course.

Researchers scored students based on self-efficacy (ready), motivation to lead (willing), and skill (able). [38]

The survey administered pre- and post-course found that, in general, students had high levels of "transactional leadership." [39] Transactional leadership is rewarding team members for a job well done, like offering feedback that helps them. Interestingly, the pre- and post-course surveys revealed a lower self-interested ("calculative") leadership motivation, with students scoring highest in transactional leadership and lowest in self-interested leadership motivation both times. [40] "Calculative" or "self-interested" simply refers to how much a person thinks about what they can gain from a leadership position.

This implies that students are cautious about an opportunistic approach, which is encouraging. Students are displaying temperance and an understanding that doing anything for the wrong reasons undercuts performance. Reduced motivation to lead could also mean that students remain modest about their leadership skills even after training. Plato and Socrates would be pleased by such humility.

Within the results, different groups had different achievements. The study reported that "students who enter the course with median levels of leadership self-efficacy make significant gains across all three areas of efficacy, skill, and motivation." [41] High-level leadership self-efficacy students boosted their leadership skills and increased their self-disinterested leadership motivation.

Even low-level leadership self-efficacy students were able to increase their self-efficacy, if nothing else. The data shows that leadership skills can be developed, though for some parties, it may take more time. This should be enough for any aspiring philosopher king to add some much-needed order to their life.

Criticizing Plato's philosopher king

Although his utopian society is attractive, Plato cannot escape the holes that class structure and rulership place in it. In particular, the Noble Lie can be a bitter pill to swallow, presenting the idea that instead of being educated to take over certain roles in the city, we should be told we were formed on the earth and some people were born better than others, mixed with gold and silver versus the more common metals. Whatever metal you were determined your municipal role. [42]

Omitting educational progress in favor of presenting virtues as innate provided a stronger and more insidious call to action. That is, if you become something through education, you could still choose to become something else. However, if you were *born* something, you could not escape it and had no choice but to fulfill your duties. Socrates felt that the lie was better than the truth, that it was "noble" because it resulted in a functioning city. (It's helpful to tap into a utilitarian sentiment here to understand what he is getting at: "The needs of the many outweigh the needs of the few.") [43]

Another related issue, already mentioned, is that the city's happiness does not (and *need* not) translate to personal happiness. Given their connection, doing one's duties to the state should aid in doing one's duties for the soul, but completely neglecting one's personal needs at all times is an unrealistic path to personal fulfillment.

Also, many believe that kingship is too much power for one person. With so many people involved, any misstep would have drastic results. Corruption becomes an even graver concern, especially if there's too much red tape to cross to depose the compromised leader.

Lastly, the rarity objection. If most philosophers are useless as Adeimantus claims, then what exactly are we left with?

Plato would not have been too concerned about the neglect of personal happiness, believing it occurred naturally through care for the state. But *we* should be. The city can't possibly care for each individual, and no matter how regulated a soul is, things will happen to disrupt it. Therefore, neglecting personal needs is a grave ramification, indeed.

The only appropriate response to this objection is *don't*. We needn't follow Plato on each whim, and personal care is and always has been very important.

Kingships are likely too much power for one person, evidenced by the existence of constitutional monarchies that use checks and balances (like the British monarchy). While limiting power in this way has been helpful for nations and societies, one question remains–in situations where we still *do* need individual leaders, how do we train them, so they don't fall corrupt?

If 70% of leadership is rooted in experience as the Keating, Rosch, and Burgoon study cited earlier claimed, then educating leaders would be just a matter of time. While Plato might have been overzealous in his model of grooming philosopher kings, some of his chosen qualities remain helpful in general preparation for leadership, including "good memory, quick apprehension" and "[being] akin to truth." Perhaps accompanying these could be a love of learning and a self-disinterested sort of ambition. Even if you don't want to be a leader, these qualities still cast a very focused net over ways you can improve your critical thinking ability.

Thanks to Plato's enduring value, people are still putting a spin on his ideas. Journalist Walter Lippmann argued that modern democracy could use a Platonist-inspired intervention, positing in *Public Opinion* that "the real environment is altogether too big, too complex, and too fleeting for direct acquaintance." [44] In other words, people lacked the capability to fully understand their work, which especially applied to those in government.

The solution, Lippmann thought, was to call in an expert, disinterested outside party to reveal to politicians the blind spots they missed, offering a truly objective account that couldn't be replicated by anyone closely involved. [45] This hearkens back to Plato in an intriguing way. If some of his ideas are hard to apply, then at least we can understand through Lippmann and others why they need to be articulated. Unfortunately, Plato's world was not perfect, and neither is ours.

Action Steps

As philosopher king, you will want to exercise your skills in temperance, courage, and wisdom for the good of your soul. Here are some questions you can ask to apply these cardinal virtues to your life.

Temperance

1. In what ways are you immoderate (too much food, too little sleep, binge-watching)?
2. What consequences do these have on your life?
3. Can you commit to half of your current intake? A quarter?

Courage

1. What is something that you have been avoiding?
2. How can you take a step toward completing this task today?
3. Can you devise an overall plan for completion—and stick to it?

Wisdom

1. Which belief do you cling to most?

2. Look up a rebuttal to this specific view. Take it in —in its entirety.
3. Think out a response to the rebuttal. If detailed, write it down.

Moving On

At the beginning of the chapter, we encountered a hopeful answer as to whether all leaders were doomed to be corrupt. Research indicates that leadership is mostly experience and that strengthening people's leadership skills through education does have an effect. Specifically, the students in the 2008 study had tested low in self-interested motivation to lead, even after completing the leadership course. This makes our prognosis following past corruption very hopeful indeed.

Chapter Summary

- Despite anecdotal evidence, not all rulers eventually become corrupt.
- Plato coded the philosopher king "gold" in his Noble Lie. Their function was to lead society with reason.
- The military class ("silver") led with courage, and the producers ("bronze and iron") were temperate.
- Together, the three classes comprised the three parts of the soul (reason, emotion, and appetite)

and created justice when each was at peak performance and led by a wise king.
- Philosopher kings had to be strictly educated in stories, gymnastics, and truth.
- Research proves that leadership is mostly learned, thus extending it to everyone.

8

AN ETHICAL INQUIRY

HOW CARDINAL VALUES KEEP THE SOUL HEALTHY

Virtue (aretê) is not something we tend to stop and think about these days, unless it's intersected with pop culture as with Jiminy Cricket from *Pinocchio*. (As the song from the 1940 film goes, "always let your conscience be your guide.") [1] Plato, on the other hand, pondered virtue extensively throughout his lifetime.

The shorter, early dialogues were usually devoted to a single concept such as the "Euthyphro," which pondered piety, or the courage-oriented "Laches." Plato's relatives Charmides and Critias showed up in the "Charmenides," a deliberation regarding temperance. [2] Though the dialogue takes place when they were quite young, both Charmides and Critias later became associated with the Thirty's extreme tactics. (Perhaps they should have listened better to Socrates.)

Early dialogues reached for firm definitions yet sometimes failed. [3] The "Republic," a middle work, features stories and symbolism in the "Ring of Gyges," the "Allegory of the Cave," and the "Myth of Er." Where earlier works focused on other virtues, like temperance and courage, the "Republic" mainly tackled justice but also examined virtue on the whole.

In the "Republic," Plato claimed that living a just and virtuous life would get you to eudaemonia. As remote as such a concept is, it remarkably has turned up in scientific studies.

A 2013 study on human gene expression profiles differentiated between "hedonic" and "eudaemonic" well-being. [4] Hedonic well-being relates to hedonism or pleasure-seeking. This type of happiness usually doesn't last and is considered lesser than eudaemonic well-being—a happiness accompanied by virtue and, hence, long-term flourishing.

Acting on former studies that "show a systematic shift in basal gene expression profiles during extended periods of stress, threat, or uncertainty," (through inflammation and fewer antibodies), the study looked at around 21,000 genes in 80 adults for both types of well-being. [5]

Hedonism and eudaemonia were measured by sample characteristics, including history of alcohol use (higher with the former) and lack of mental health problems (displayed by both types). [6] Though similar, the two can be differentiated by overlapping characteristics. (Lack of depression plus significant alcohol use likely implies hedonic well-being, for example.) Higher regulation of a "stress-related conserved transcriptional response to adversity (CTRA)" in gene expression accompanied hedonistic well-being,[7] while eudaemonia was defined by just the opposite: lower regulation of the same response.[8]

The higher physical maintenance of hedonistic well-being seems to confirm that such happiness is usually temporary and not sustainable for long periods of time as eudaemonistic well-being is. However, eudaemonia is more difficult to achieve. The study found that just a little over one-fifth of the participants exhibited higher eudaemonistic well-being than hedonistic, proving its relative rarity.[9]

If eudaemonia is characterized by lower regulation of the stress response, implying less physical work, then why isn't it easier to come by? Perhaps because the challenge of *maintaining* eudaemonia is more difficult than simply reaching it. Getting to a long-term happy, settled state is much harder than a hedonistic jaunt through your favorite guilty pleasure. Although this takes some work, the result of deeper life satisfaction and joy is worth it.

Plato's path to eudaemonia lies in cultivating four cardinal virtues. Delving further into his code of ethics, we see how important virtue is in becoming happier long-term and living a more fulfilling life.

Introducing Plato's ethics

Plato's ethics involved keeping the soul and society well-fed by acting justly and in accordance with three other qualities: wisdom, courage, and temperance. Only by living a life of virtue could a person reach eudaemonia, a flourishing state. (Eudaemonia is often translated as "happiness," but "satisfaction" is more accurate.)

While speaking with Glaucon in the dialogue, Socrates made a point about power corrupting everyone through an anecdote involving a golden ring that made the wearer invisible, called the "Ring of Gyges." [10] Glaucon had argued that the wearer would always take advantage of the invisibility by robbing, murdering, and sleeping with whomever he wanted. Anyone who could do something and get away with it would keep doing it… otherwise, he was a fool. Thus, it was better to be unjust than just. [11]

Plato devoted much of the "Republic's" remainder to refuting Glaucon's "Ring of Gyges" argument. He eventually showed that no worldly good, even a magical ring, could compete with the happiness resulting from a healthy soul.

This ring (and the possibility of misbehavior while using it) ties into Plato's idea of the just man. Justice relates to virtue, which is defined as an "excellence of everything for which a specific work or function is appointed." [12] In other words, virtue is a state of functioning well, and anything that functions well possesses virtue. Justice, then, is "excellence or virtue of soul." [13]

To achieve justice, or excellence of soul, you needed the three other cardinal virtues: wisdom, courage, and temperance. [14] These virtues meant a well-regulated soul, which in turn meant discovering eudaemonia. Later associated with Aristotle, eudaemonia is a state of contentment brought about by excellence of functioning (or virtue).

By limiting interest to worldly goods and acting unjustly, Glaucon's ring-wearer would miss out on eudaemonia because their soul would be chaotic and disorderly from following all the wrong impulses or even following the right ones to excess. Using a ring to take advantage of people not only isn't right, but as it turns out, it isn't very good for you.

Plato's four cardinal virtues of justice, wisdom, courage, and temperance unlock eudaemonia. A tentative definition of justice has already been offered. How, then, are we meant to understand the other three?

The three other virtues

Plato identified wisdom as the "science of guardianship or government," effectively limiting it to the ruling class. [15] He ruled out specialized knowledge in other areas like metalworking and agriculture. [16] Oddly enough, philosophical education didn't seem to make the cut in this definition.

Courage, he insisted, was "the conservation of the conviction which the law has created by education about fearful things." [17] He added that a brave person doesn't let pain or fear influence their actions.

Unpacking the quote, Socrates is referring to the perspective that soldiers had to (and still must) adopt to fight effectively. The law needed to cling to them "like a dye." [18] Specifically, the law's assessment of what was to be feared informed how the soldiers navigated within that fear to survive. This could be accomplished by learning about the thing causing the fear and how to vanquish it.

Temperance is "the concord of the naturally superior and inferior as to which ought to rule both in the state and the individual." [19] The broadness of this definition makes it easy for individuals to fill in the blanks, as overindulgence and underindulgence can occur with just about anything. Distinct from the separate virtues of wisdom and bravery, temperance lay behind all other virtues, "bringing about the unison in the same chant of the strongest, the weakest and the intermediate." [20]

Thus, the cardinal virtues interact with temperance filtering through the other two. As Aristotle would later argue in his "Indoctrine of the Mean," courage is the middle ground between cowardice and foolhardiness and, therefore, a type of temperance. [21] Courage, temperance, and wisdom together create justice.

Reasoning through decisions

Reason is a large component of decision-making, as we saw in Chapter 7. However, Plato's stance that emotion should be governed by reason opposes that of modern scholars who contend that the roles they play in decision-making are closer to equal and that reason alone isn't enough.

In fact, both reason *and* emotion work together in different areas of the brain to form a decision. The prefrontal cortex in the brain "anticipates the costs and benefits of our actions, and utilizes information about past experiences to regulate behavior" while the limbic system "assists in the affective evaluation of rewards and losses." [22] These areas collaborate in solid decision-making.

The rational part of good decision-making necessitates taking note of all possible consequences of an action. Expected utility theory (EUT) developed by Daniel Bernoulli in the early eighteenth century [23] postulates that "the value of an alternative consists of the sum of the utilities of its outcomes, each weighed by probability." [24] In other words, the role reason plays under this lens in decision-making is to leave no stone unturned and follow each premise to its natural conclusion. Knowing all your options will lead to a better-supported decision. The more you exercise your mind, Plato claimed, the better decisions you will make. Factoring in emotional intelligence makes for the best decisions of all.

Moderation is also important. As noted in the previous section, temperance is good for its own sake and also makes courage, wisdom, and justice easier to obtain through its resounding focus on balance. A balanced life leads to virtue and increased contentment, its sustainability lasting longer than hedonistic pleasures.

The philosopher king from the last chapter ties it all together, leading the three classes with wisdom. The perfect judgment of this philosopher king, cultivated by years of education, would lead his subjects to the justice of a society that excels and is virtuous. (Yet remember that according to modern science, emotion plays a greater role in our lives than Plato would like to admit.)

Action Steps

Reaching eudaemonia can be a challenge, as research shows. Still, Plato's claim that virtue leads to eudaemonia is intuitive and, given the upsides of a happy life, worth trying. Take a look at the following ways you can enact virtue in your life.

1. Pick up trash (and recycling) around your neighborhood.
2. Buy a coffee for a stranger.
3. Devise two or three compliments while looking at yourself in the mirror.
4. Spend time caring for the people closest to you.
5. Volunteer in an activity of your choice.
6. Donate old books to your local library.
7. Make someone smile or laugh.

Moving On

Even in a world that doesn't encourage it, make virtue something that you stop and think about. Helping others should be a consideration, but don't forget the virtue associated with the self. It's your own happiness that you're after.

Chapter Summary

- Eudaemonic well-being is much rarer, yet richer, than hedonic well-being.
- Plato's four cardinal virtues were justice, temperance, courage, and wisdom.
- Temperance affects all other virtues that relate to balance and moderation, including courage.
- Plato claimed that a philosopher must hone their reasoning faculties to be able to lead and regulate the soul.

9

THE PERFECT SOCIETY
WHAT A PHILOSOPHER'S UTOPIA TEACHES US ABOUT GOOD GOVERNMENT IN THESE CHANGING TIMES

The implications of social class go beyond overt differences like possessions, dress, and speech: A UK web survey of 161,400 participants revealed seven distinct classes in place of Plato's three or the upper, middle, and working-class model with which most of us are accustomed. [1] These include the "elite, established middle class, technical middle class, new affluent workers, traditional working class, emergent service workers, [and] precariat." [2] The study argued, "Class operates symbolically and culturally through forms of stigmatisation and marking of personhood and value." [3]

A nationally representative survey of 1,062 participants by the same group measured each class represented by size, in which the elite came in smallest at 6% just as Plato had theorized. [4] Fifty-six percent of the elite surveyed were graduates, a greater percentage than any of the other classes. [5] This, too, echoes Plato's idea of an educated higher class.

Plato's societal ideas, therefore, are represented to some extent in the real world. Class structure in the "Republic," Plato's most-studied work, will be further explored here in a deeper reading of the dialogue. His theories regarding education, politics, and society hold value for today's society, as do the critiques that arise regarding them.

Overview and themes of the "Republic"

As Plato's most eminent work, the "Republic" is iconic in ethics, metaphysics, and epistemology. It spans ten books (chapters) and targets education, politics, and justice, in particular. Scholars believe the first book was written before the other nine because of its similarity to early dialogues, which explains differences in structure and content.

Cephalus, an elderly Athenian with three sons also in the dialogue (Lysias, Euthydemus, and Polemarchus), got the ball rolling in Book 1, [6] commenting on aging and higher sensitivity regarding past wrongs. Possessing wealth, the "good man" would refrain from doing bad things, he said, so that he didn't die in literal or moral debt. [7] This led to a discussion on justice.

In Book 2, Socrates asserted that justice was intrinsically and extrinsically valuable. That is, justice is valuable in and of itself and for its results. [8] Glaucon then presented the "Ring of Gyges" to illustrate that acting unjustly is more advantageous than acting justly. After that, perhaps inspired by the Forms, Socrates shifted focus to justice in an entire city as opposed to a single person's soul. [9] This city forms the scope of the current chapter.

Socrates presented "The Noble Lie" in Book 3 to keep everybody working on their respective virtues so that the city could run, discussing the four cardinal virtues and seeking them first in the city and then in the soul. He offered a three-part model for both in Book 4. [10]

From there, Socrates went in a more radical direction. If we abolished the family unit and raised children in common, Socrates argued, then that would make it easier to keep the children's focus on the state, especially through education. [11] Excellence would only occur in the right environment. [12]

Not everyone has the stamina for rule. Comparing the city to a ship and its ruler to a shipmaster in Book 6 in the "Ship of State," Socrates spoke of a group of rowdy, mutinous sailors trying to get to the helm. He declared that the only person fit to take them on was the seasoned philosopher king. [13]

Socrates then turned to Forms with a series of scenarios. "The Analogy of the Sun" and "Analogy of the Divided Line" are detailed in Book 6, along with the "Allegory of the Cave" in Book 7. (A fuller picture of the analogies comes later in the chapter.) Afterward, he appraised five forms of government: aristocracy, timocracy, oligarchy, democracy, and tyranny in Book 8. Putting together a narrative that moved through each type becoming corrupted somehow, he ended up endorsing a philosopher king as ruler. [14]

Finally, Socrates told the Myth of Er in Book 10, depicting a recently deceased character, Er, and his path through the afterlife. Souls were judged before heaven and earth, entering those locations based on how they conducted themselves in the lives they just left. [15]

After living their afterlives for a thousand years, the souls returned from heaven and earth to be reassigned to new lives, usually choosing a different fate than before. (One from heaven chose tyranny). [16] These souls were then tasked to drink from the "River of Forgetfulness" (Lethe), although Er did not. Following this, all the souls traveled up to the sky for rebirth. [17]

<u>Assessing themes in the "Republic"</u>

Three of the most important recurring themes in the "Republic" are education, politics, and justice. Each impacts society and the self, molding you into your best existence in Plato's view.

<u>Education</u>

Already touched upon briefly, discussions related to education for philosophers and philosopher kings took up a good deal of the dialogue. Plato recommended music and gymnastics in early education and telling fables to young children to provide moral direction. (Today, this might look like telling your kids about Santa punishing bad children by not giving them presents). Fables also prepared children to receive facts later on through symbolic similarity.

Approaching adulthood, the more promising children would be taught philosophy and how to run a government, but Plato cautioned against educating the wrong types of people for leadership. Students could not be too sensitive or aggressive or they were corruptible, causing more harm in future office than good.

Politics (the government shuffle)

The five types of government named by Plato were aristocracy, timocracy, oligarchy, democracy, and tyranny.

Plato named aristocracy "the government of the best, whom we aver to the truly good and just man," [18] presenting it as ideal rulership, with education creating better rulers. [19] Supporting this, Merriam-Webster defines aristocracy as "a government in which power is vested in a minority consisting of those believed to be best qualified." [20] When one well-qualified person holds power, their government is called a monarchy; if there are multiple rulers, then it's an aristocracy. [21]

Aristocracy (ideal), timocracy (less ideal), and oligarchy (unideal)

Plato showed how justice could fail in the city by discussing the five government types and the men corresponding to each type. He endorsed aristocracy alone and identified four defective forms of government, beginning with the decline of aristocracy into timocracy.

According to the time of year, some births were more sanctioned by the gods than others. Plato cited a bizarre calculation involving augmentations, distances, and limits that arrived at a "perfect number." The first decline occurred when a ruler deviated from this supposedly-divine formula and his children were born flawed, creating a flaw in future leadership. [22]

The flawed generation strayed from the careful process that went into educating rulers, shunning music in particular, and was therefore unable to properly sort and direct the different classes. Thus, the metals comprising these classes (as told in the "Noble Lie") got intermingled and waged war on one another, weakening the government. [23] This took a just aristocracy down to timocracy, a system built around honor.

Timocracy echoed the aristocracy in honoring rulers and knowledge of warfare. However, since all the wise men were now made of mixed metal (according to belief), they appeared untrustworthy, and people were reluctant to elect them. This prompted the subsequent degeneration. Switching from the government type to the type of person (and more particularly the state of their soul), [24] the timocrat was also more spirited and, unlike the aristocrat, of the notion that war was honorable over peace. He began to dip into his appetites and lust for money, a precursor to oligarchy. [25] Thus, the honor-bound society looked the wrong way for virtue, with the wrong person leading the way.

Socrates noted that the timocrat's father had been reluctant to take necessary action against wrongdoers, "willing to forbear something of his rights in order to escape trouble." Perhaps this was his imagining of honor, not unlike pacifists avoiding violence on principle. [26] The timocrat had watched his father refuse to prosecute debtors because he considered it "meddling" and was encouraged by his mother and house-slaves to take action against them when grown. [27]

This sentiment permeated an entire generation, where apparent backlash toward parents resulted in support for taking action–an honored deed–and condemnation for refraining from interfering in other people's affairs. [28] Still fond of wealth, the timocrat kept accumulating and even "pervert[ed] the laws" to spend money until greed outpaced love of honor. Everybody jumped on the bandwagon, pushing timocracy into oligarchy. [29]

When money overtook education and honor as markers of sophistication and competence, the oligarchy was born. Rich, greedy property owners ruled the city, laying down a financial threshold for office, and governmental affairs worsened as lack of proper qualification meant things were poorly run. The oligarchs' corruption spread to the rest of the people over time, especially as they refused to donate to needier folks. [30] The endless quest for wealth and exclusion of the poor drove the city further into poverty, creating the presence of "beggars" and "cutpurses" and toppling the oligarchy into democracy. [31]

Democracy's "freedom for all"

Democracy occurred "when the poor, winning the victory, put to death some of the other party, [drove] out others, and grant[ed] the rest of the citizens an equal share in citizenships and offices." [32] Liberty and freedom of speech were two key tenets that Socrates identified, along with the common ability to hold office and participate in juries. [33]

Returning to the personified idea of government as soul, the democratic soul arose from the oligarchal one due to the reign of property owners necessarily devolving into majority rule after the poor rebelled. The democrat (and democracy by extension) was at war with himself due to conflicting appetites: wealth and liberty. A poor education was propped up by "false and braggart words and opinions," and he would not listen to the wiser words of his elders. [34] The democrat dealt in conflicts and thumbed his nose at moderation. Socrates also argued that democrats ascribed positive meanings to negative traits: insolence masqueraded under the name of "good breeding," license "liberty," prodigality "magnificence," and shamelessness "manly spirit." [35]

The democrat believed all appetites were the same and worth following, said Socrates, and promoted liberty for everyone. Students were as free as teachers, and parents as free as children. (Here, Socrates asserted, a hierarchical relationship was necessary for any learning to occur.) This "freedom for all" approach created instability, and when citizens were so spoiled by it, they opted not to follow the laws. This left the door open for the worst government of all. [36]

Unveiling the tyrant

When times were bad, the population of a democracy tended to "put forward one man as its special champion and protector and cherish and magnify him." [37] And so the protector was born with the power of popular support.

According to Socrates, the protector became condemned to tyranny in "tast[ing] of the one bit of human entrails minced up with those of other victims" and turning into a wolf; in a more literal sense, this might look like restraining a mob and unfairly picking someone to put to death as mob leader as Socrates outlined. [38] Much like a related myth involving lycanthropy (turning into a werewolf), the blood on his hands turned the protectorate's character irreversibly. [39] Political leaders could not avoid this moral turpitude forever, as such circumstances came with the territory.

Eventually, the tyrant would need to request a bodyguard because people were calling for his head, a result of "always stirring up some war so that the people may be in need of a leader." [40] Forced to get rid of everybody who disagreed with him, the tyrant soon had no one left, which, along with resource depletion, would mean being forced to leave the city in disgrace. [41]

This story of governmental deterioration depicts a simultaneous decline of justice, ending with the eternal imprisonment of a soul beneath the Earth. The connection to the Myth of Er will be explored in the following section.

Justice

Justice is the most studied theme in the "Republic," and Plato showed how we can use it to live our best lives by his reckoning. As we know, justice is the "excellence or virtue of soul," and also of a city. [42] It can be achieved only by honoring the virtues of courage, temperance, and wisdom. In the soul, wisdom should lead to courage and temperance so that this fourth virtue may follow, which is how individuals reach eudaemonia.

Plato developed his idea of justice over the course of the "Republic." In Book 1, Thrasymachus opined that justice was "the advantage of the stronger," [43] which Socrates deflected by noting that an action isn't just simply because no one knows about it or you have an army and can fight your way out of it being thought unjust. [44] He added that in its ideal state, political office was designed for leaders to act in their subjects' interest rather than their own, which protects the *less* powerful party. [45]

These are important distinctions to make. The first counterargument challenges the overly simplistic view that "might is right," and the second evokes a key tenet of democracy: the right of the minority. (However, Socrates seemed to sidestep the fact that rulers *do* act in their own self-interest quite often and that no one is enforcing the ideal.)

Glaucon reluctantly offered the "Ring of Gyges" myth in Book 2 to support the case for injustice. [46] Afterward, Socrates tackled Thrasymachus' claim that injustice held greater rewards than justice. [47] He kept at this topic through the rest of the work.

In Book 4, Socrates described justice in the city as minding your work only and not interfering with the two other classes. [48] This distinguished it from justice of the soul, which required intermingling of the parts. It took, therefore, a philosopher king and a healthy dose of specialization for justice to settle upon the city.

Scenarios corresponding to proper leadership in the city, the Forms, and education followed with the "Ship of State" and the "Allegory of the Cave" in Books 6 and 7.

The end of the "Republic" brought the focus back to justice. The governmental shuffle into depravity in Book 8 tied into the Myth of Er, which relayed that acting unjustly would put you below the earth for 1,000 years and that acting *too* unjustly would trap you there. Tyrants, in particular, did not get to come back to be reborn. [49] Socrates used the Myth of Er to illustrate the perils of being unjust as well as the rewards of justice in the afterlife: eudaemonia and a balanced soul.

<u>Return of the Forms</u>

Plato's Theory of Forms resurfaced in the "Analogy of the Sun," the "Analogy of the Divided Line," and the "Allegory of the Cave." While an entire chapter has been devoted to Plato's "Allegory of the Cave," the two analogies have not yet been covered.

Picking up on the "Cave Allegory," in which former cave dwellers would eventually be able to gaze at the Sun, the "Analogy of the Sun" explained that vision required a source of illumination. Plato analogized sunlight on a visible object to the Form of Goodness's offspring (since the Sun is not vision itself) shining on truth: If the soul was not focused correctly, it could not see truth or be able to reason. [50]

Analogy of the Divided Line
4 Levels of Reality

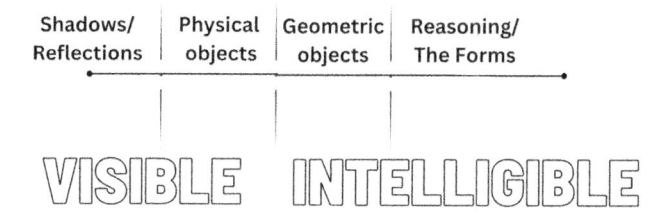

Shadows/ Reflections	Physical objects	Geometric objects	Reasoning/ The Forms

VISIBLE | **INTELLIGIBLE**

"The Analogy of the Divided Line" began with a line cut unequally, and those two lines were cut again to form four pieces. The size of the respective sections represented how real they were, and only the middle two were equal. [51] The two leftmost pieces were the visible sections. These were less reliable reflections of reality, according to Plato. The rightmost two were the intelligible sections, or what we could reason with the mind. These were more reliable. [52]

The leftmost visible piece made likenesses of things we see, such as shadows and reflections, so they were considered least reliable. The larger visible section to its right included *actual* things we see, a little more reliable but still not comprising knowledge. [53] Ideas made up the intelligible sections: geometric shapes and numbers comprised the third piece, and the rightmost (longest) fourth section was reasoning and dialect related to the Forms. Plato designated these aspects of reality as more real and knowable than visible objects, with the Forms as the most real of all. [54] (Interestingly, things we see, and geometric objects were equal pieces, but only the latter was granted the title of "knowledge.")

These Analogies and the "Allegory of the Cave" have a common theme: all three superimpose Forms over the reality we see, insisting that Forms are the true reality. Socrates claimed that the reflection of an object in the water is a likeness, but the object itself is a likeness of the Form. [55]

In the "Cave Allegory" Socrates set up an alternate setting to compare to that which we understood as reality. The "Analogy of the Sun" provided a more relatable image of a sunbeam on a visible object to denote Goodness shining on the truth. But the most thorough examination was the "Analogy of the Divided Line," which appraised four levels of reality and again endorsed Forms at the very top.

Criticism and modern appraisal

These days, the "Republic" is commonly criticized. It is called too elitist, as well as also bigoted and racist. Certain parts seem to call for eugenics. To top it off, placing democracy one step above tyranny rankles quite a few critics, as well.

As one critic colorfully put it, Plato was "a reactionary resolutely opposed to every principle of the liberal creed." [56] Modern philosopher Karl Popper referred to the ruling class as a "master race," calling the Noble Lie "precisely analogous to the Nazi doctrine of blood and soil." [57] (Blood designated a nationalistic Aryan race, while soil represented settlement for these chosen individuals.) [58] Considering Plato's talk about the proper time and place to breed philosopher kings, his allusion to xenophobic stereotypes [59] and his belief in Greek superiority, [60] such accusations, though dramatic, were not far off base.

Some were softer in their approach. In its chapter targeting elitism in Plato and Aristotle, the *Cambridge Companion to Ancient Ethics* opens with the following: "It is an old and persistent complaint about ancient ethics that it is unjustifiably elitist, that is, that it restricts the possibility of virtue to too narrow a group. And since ancient ethics tightly links happiness to virtue, the possibility of happiness is similarly restricted." [61]

Pointing out that most people won't achieve aretê (virtue) *or* eudaemonia, the introduction unveils a stronger concern regarding moral capability. This may be because reaching eudaemonia is more or less up to ourselves but most of us want to believe that everyone has a baseline capability so at least they have a shot. Though Plato seemed more optimistic about capability in his later dialogues, his "cognitive demands [...] on the virtuous agent [...], when combined with differing intellectual capabilities among people, are a main source of Plato's elitism." [62]

Compared to the flashier (but perhaps more dated) Nazi master race charge, the elitism accusation has stuck around longer. Socrates named dying as his greatest philosophical achievement, thus ridding himself of his bodily appetites. This is asking a lot of his would-be philosopher kings; we are to keep our souls in check with regular study, but only in approved disciplines and perfect moderation in all aspects of our lives. Recall that Socrates called for raising children in common, creating semantic difficulties (what to call communal guardians if "Mom" or "Dad" seems too intimate) to say nothing of psychological ones. We are only human, and Plato is easy to understand but harder to implement.

The interpretations of racism and elitism in Plato's "Republic" are legitimate. Anti-democratic is another fair label, given what Socrates had to say about it. Plato wasn't much one for freedom. As relayed earlier in the chapter, he had Socrates go through its key tenets and cynically translate them into less desirable traits. Plato named liberty "license," which indicates boldness and a lack of entitlement for what is asked. Thus, anti-democratic joins other labels racism, elitism (and perhaps bigotry as well) in being harsh but fair assessments of the ideas shared in the "Republic." As scholar John H. Hallowell frankly put it, Plato "does not believe that the state comes into existence primarily for the purpose of promoting and preserving individual freedom." [63]

Failing to name these shortcomings would be a disservice to modern sensibilities. However, that doesn't mean we need to throw the baby out with the bathwater. The entirety of Plato's work has survived for a reason, and that is because encased in dated notions is a core that still lives, breathes, and inspires us.

Criticisms of Plato's ethics

In recent years, Plato's ethics have come under fire for upholding power structures that keep less fortunate people disenfranchised. John H. Hallowell declared his Noble Lie was seen as "deception through the use of propaganda," which is dramatic but perhaps accurate. [64] Propaganda is defined by Merriam-Webster as "ideas, facts, or allegations spread deliberately to further one's cause or to damage an opposing cause." [65] Since he intended the lie to support his ideal society, it fits within the parameters of propaganda.

In addition, many scholars also feel that his class system smacks of elitism and keeps power in the hands of a "privileged minority." [66] Comparisons to fascism weren't too far behind, especially in light of the state-over-individual approach and rigid socioeconomic boundaries featured in the "Republic."

These valid critiques add some resistance to adopting Plato's ethics in the modern day. In particular, after observing the political careers of Hitler and Mussolini, some of his ideas leave a bitter aftertaste. A deeper treatment of Plato's critics follows in the next chapter.

The elitism implied in the Noble Lie runs a little close to Aristotle's natural slave concept. However, where Plato argued (through the lie) that some people were born to rule, Aristotle proclaimed that some people were born to be enslaved. These ideas are dangerous and dehumanizing, intent on using people as a mere means to an end.

Keeping marginalized populations down is an untenable approach in the modern day. Plato's eagerness to assign classes and pressure people to stay within them should give readers pause. People of color, women, the LGBT community, and physically and mentally disabled people might still get the short end of the stick.

However, we can acknowledge these critiques of Plato's city while still keeping parts of his concept of soul. Remember that eudaemonic well-being means lower regulation of stress responses, indicating a more relaxed state. Skipping over Plato's city for now, move on to your soul. Finding your own balance and ethics will help you achieve better life satisfaction than you'll get following someone else's path.

Plato defined virtue as excellence. What are you excellent at, and what makes you happy? Focusing on innate gifts boosts self-esteem and increases the likelihood that you will share your happiness with others.

It is imperative not to take the "Republic" too literally. Perhaps Plato's greatest drawback is his ivory-tower impracticality in certain areas, having bequeathed us more than a few ideas that we can't use (and that some power-hungry people take advantage of). Luckily, he has also equipped us with sensibilities that still resonate, like knowing the value of Justice.

You can create Justice in yourself by solving altercations rather than starting them, or channel virtue by assisting others, like holding doors open for people. Keep in mind the Forms surrounding such actions. One of the best things you can do for yourself is to find your own sense of purpose that brings personal fulfillment as well as a better society. Prioritize education to foster personal growth and a keener mind, taking every opportunity to learn from a trusted source. Focus on what you can change to avoid being overwhelmed by what you can't.

A 2021 study on education suggested that preparing to teach a topic is an excellent way of learning it. Researchers gave participating students learning materials and ran two experiments, each with two groups. The first group was tested on the material, and the researchers informed the other group that they would be teaching it. The first experiment focused more on establishing teaching as a way of learning while the second required giving students more advanced age-appropriate materials to see if the principle held. [67]

Researchers grouped 206 undergraduates in the first experiment and 214 in the second between those expecting to take a test and those expecting to teach (but the teaching students did not actually have to teach, as they were later told). Giving participants readings on the Doppler effect, the researchers made another split between immediate and delayed testing. [68] Even a week after reading the materials, they found that students tasked with teaching had 9% better factual recall. [69] So teaching really does help us learn.

Action Steps

From Teaching to Mastery

Hearkening back to the *Found An Academy* exercise, this will look at teaching a concept more thoroughly. Choose your favorite concept from this book thus far: eudaemonia, virtue, justice, courage, etc. Keep it simple. How would you explain this concept to a loved one? (Grab another person for this. Unlike in the scientific study, you *will* be teaching.)

For example, if you were teaching the following well-known syllogism (two true premises leading to a conclusion), you might first consider how you might present it and contextualize it through dialogue.

1. *All men are mortal.*
2. *Socrates is a man.*

Therefore, Socrates is mortal.

Now transfer these considerations to the concept you have chosen, devising a plan for how you will go about teaching it. Set up a simple structure for a single concept to avoid overcomplicating things.

- *Tip:* You could start, as Socrates often did, by asking your "student" what the concept is and what it looks like. This encourages self-discovery and opens the door for you to ask more guiding questions. Next, determine roughly how you'll explain your perceptions to them when you are in closer agreement regarding the concept.

When you've figured out your mini-lecture, say it out loud to yourself. You should feel confident and competent on the topic. Now go and talk it over with your "student."

- *Tip:* Concentrate chiefly on the process of explanation and your level of comfort with the topic while speaking about it but keep abreast of their responses in order to bridge their insights to yours. Often, someone else will pick up on something you haven't even considered.

Afterward, check in with yourself. Did teaching and discussing the concept lead to any gained comprehension?

The teaching-learning cycle keeps your mind active, and preparing something as though you're going to teach it is a great way to demystify a concept you're having trouble with.

Moving On

The technique above goes hand-in-hand with Plato's teaching at the Academy as well as his dialogue format. Most of his ideas are enduring. However, of everything Plato espoused in the "Republic," his three-class system tends to stick most with people because, as the research shows, we still tend to put a lot of clout in social class.

Yet Plato's virtue-driven city is everything we don't want, from gaslighting citizens into believing they were born to municipal duties (and thus anchored to them) to taking children away from their birth families also for the good of the city. His anti-democratic perspective has filtered through to the disillusioned the world over, who now put their stock in authoritarian leaders.

Ironically this democratic backsliding, also seen in America, [70] circles back to Plato's condemnation of tyranny, revealing the double edge of adopting Platonic tenets today. On the one hand, his disdain for democracy may have helped inspire authoritarian rule, but on the other hand, that authoritarianism created a state of government he liked even *less*—just like he said it would.

It seems Plato had no solution, merely the power of discussing one. However, the complications of adapting him for modern use are offset by unmistakable personal and societal benefits, including in the courtroom, as we'll see in the next chapter.

Chapter Summary

- Plato's most famous work, the "Republic," discusses justice throughout.
- Proper education of future philosopher kings would be integral to good rulership and include guidance in governance and reasoning.
- The "Ship of State" chronicled mutinous sailors and asserted that only a philosopher could gain control over them.
- Five forms of government are named: aristocracy, timocracy, oligarchy, democracy, and tyranny, with aristocracy the favorite and tyranny the most dreaded.
- The "Analogy of the Sun" and "Analogy of the Divided Line" illustrated the power of Forms and presented them as truer than the forms we physically see.
- While Plato cannot escape the charges of elitism, racism, and anti-democratic sentiments, his emphasis on education can still be useful to modern readers.

10

ECHOES OF PLATO

HOW PLATO'S INSIGHTS SHAPE MODERN DISCIPLINES AND INFLUENCE THE WAY WE THINK TODAY

Apart from his faults, Plato got many things right, with readers still flocking to his "Allegory of the Cave" and his call to lead the soul with reason. While he and Socrates kept strict parameters on how to live their lives, we have the luxury of picking and choosing which tenets we want to adopt. There is something in Plato for everybody, which the survival of his works can attest to.

Plato's dialogue format may have aimed at finding truth, but it also works as a wholesome social activity. This and other factors of the laid-back Mediterranean lifestyle were appraised in a large study published in 2023. It indicated that living our lives like Plato (within reason) has the benefit of warding off chronic diseases. One hundred and ten thousand, seven hundred and ninety-nine people took a questionnaire based on the Mediterranean Lifestyle (MEDLIFE) index that asked about diet along with "physical activity, rest, and social habits and conviviality," [1] the latter two relating to the social environment Socrates and Plato created through teaching and dialogue. Plato even encouraged conviviality with the "Symposium," which involved drinking and socializing, although philosophy, of course, was the main aim.

This easy-yet-engaged setting was exactly what the study was tracking. 9.4 years after the initial survey, researchers discovered that 2401 participants died of cancer while 731 succumbed to cardiovascular disease. Those taking a Mediterranean approach to "physical activity, rest, and social habits and conviviality" fared best in fending off cancer and cardiovascular disease, scoring 28% lower on cancer mortality and 29% lower on death overall [2].

These findings demonstrate our social needs, and it is nice to see a philosopher's lifestyle scientifically supported. Knowing the best techniques for inquiry, Plato potently combined social and educational approaches with his Academy and chronicling of Socrates' social habits. Considering that Plato died at 80 and Socrates at 70 back before modern medicine (and Socrates did not meet a natural end), there do seem to be some benefits to a Mediterranean lifestyle. Perhaps we can improve our lifestyles by being social with friends and being more inquiring when in their trusted company.

Systematic philosophy and Forms

"Western philosophy is just a series of footnotes to Plato," the mathematician Alfred North Whitehead once said [3], and indeed, Plato's influence cannot be overstated. Most philosophers, dead or alive, named him as an influence on some level, and therefore much of modern philosophy is in response to ideas raised in his dialogues. Even Aristotle, hugely influential in his own right, was taught by Plato and ideologically exists in response to Plato. Plato's impact on critical thinking and relevance in contemporary society has already done much to make us better thinkers, and we can lean on this ability with further education.

Leaning on his reasoning abilities, Plato pioneered systematic philosophy with his personal brand, Platonism, "a profound and wide-ranging" system that samples epistemology and metaphysics and features a strong focus on ethics [4]. Although systems philosophy officially debuted with Ervin László in 1974 and further developed with Ludwig von Bertalanffy's systems theory [5], Plato's work offered a prototype of the discipline. A "system" is named such because it is solid and broad enough to be applicable to scientific principles. Systematic philosophy is thus referred to as a "philosophy of nature," positing that organisms and non-living things are categorized by the "laws of organization" that define the system [6]. In short, systematic philosophy is the perspective shift that comes from adopting systems in the manner noted [7].

Plato was one of the first known philosophers to place critical thinking under a systematic lens, building up a pattern of observation, reasoning, and discussion that can lead us to the truth. Dogged inquiry and dialogue gave us a blueprint for assessing knowledge, virtue, and the nature of things, with the only true knowledge, he argued, being knowledge of the Forms, a discussion that began as Socrates lay dying. Plato devised a system to understand these three concepts better.

But appropriate knowledge acquisition can't form without solid reasoning, Plato cautioned, or the ability to say "I don't know." Only by leading with reason in the soul, always asking questions, and keenly observing the tangible and intangible elements of human existence can a person rightly come by knowledge. Plato did not go as far as to argue that reason should always trump feelings or appetites, but it should always be in control of them. He even depicted Socrates embracing his death because it would rid him of the feelings and appetites of his earthly existence, leaving his soul to pure reason. His focus on reason and his drawn connections between reason, critical thinking, and arriving at the truth spurred a ratiocentric tradition that still prevails in modern philosophy.

Like the rest of Plato's philosophy, the Theory of Forms painted a broad stroke across disciplines. It influenced how we view ideals, especially as depicted in the "Allegory of the Cave," the "Analogy of the Sun," and the "Analogy of the Divided Line." The abstract nature of the allegory and analogies make for a wide berth regarding interpretation. Martin Heidegger believed the "Cave Allegory" meant finding freedom, while Hannah Arendt took a political slant examining the implications of such "freedom."

Whether or not finding the Forms means finding freedom, they still inspire many readers to look to their ideals on the path to personal truth. (However, the Forms also dictated a certain level of removal from the physical world that is unachievable for most, making it imperative that ideals are used in measured doses.) Starting with Plato and Socrates, philosophers continue to debate what should be considered real, what is and isn't knowable, and where truth can be found.

Political philosophy and modern justice

Plato developed political philosophy in addition to systematic philosophy, a fitting progression since his background in public affairs meant that he could write convincingly about politics. His societal structure and ordering of government may not be in practice anywhere, but plenty of people still discuss them in a theoretical sense. Perhaps the closest thing we have to Plato's societal setup is India's traditional five-class caste system: Brahmins ("priests, teachers"), Kshatriyas ("warriors, rulers"), Vaishyas ("merchants, farmers, traders"), Shudras ("laborers"), and Dalits ("outcasts") [8]. Categorizing people based on occupation, this system is over 3,000 years old (even older than the "Republic") [9].

No matter the class, however, Plato expected his citizens to fulfill their duties to the city-state. Fast forward to the 20th century when John F. Kennedy said, "Ask not what your country can do for you; ask what you can do for your country" [10], which echoes Plato's zeal as he laid out a citizen's duties to their city-state. Recall that justice in a state is achieved with each class sticking to their one cardinal virtue: for the military this was courage, related to the spirit, while the producers tackled temperance over their appetites, and the ruling class produced wisdom from the rational part of the soul.

Courage is still associated with modern militaries, and good politicians still pursue wisdom in governance. Plato may have anticipated the rule of the wealthy that grips portions of our world today–even possibly the United States. A 2014 Princeton study ran surveys between 1981 and 2002 on "public policy issues" and found that "when a majority of citizens disagrees with economic elites and/or with organized interests, they generally lose" [11], [12]. This sounds like the rule of a privileged, wealthy few.

But thankfully, justice turns up in modern legal and political contexts all the time. (Just look at the social justice movements that arose in response to elite privilege and income inequality) [13]. Merriam-Webster defines justice as "the maintenance or administration of what is just especially by the impartial adjustment of conflicting claims or the assignment of merited rewards or punishments" [14]. The first part, "maintenance or administration," aligns with Plato's idea that a properly run city creates justice through other cardinal virtues. "Merited rewards or punishments" sounds a lot like the Myth of Er and the case for leading a just life.

Plato still makes appearances in the courtroom, as well. Romer v. Evans (1993) was "the first serious intervention of classics into the realm of laws," according to Jeffrey Carnes [15], targeting Colorado's Amendment 2, which banned the state and even its municipalities from creating anti-discrimination laws for the LGBT community. When people rightfully protested it under the First Amendment (prohibiting religious discrimination), moral philosopher John Finnis came in to "prove" that anti-gay sentiments were not limited to Christian roots. Ancient Greece's pederasty problem had Finnis fighting an uphill battle from the beginning. He offered a clunky and moralized account claiming that Plato (and other Greeks) found homosexuality shameful. Anything outside of marriage for procreative purposes was "sodomy and masturbation" to Plato (and Socrates) and Aristotle, Finnis argued, putting an odd Catholic bent on their arguments [16].

Then someone else came to Plato's rescue. Renowned philosopher Martha Nussbaum asserted, in response to some apparent squeamishness from Plato regarding gay sex that Finnis had picked up on, that Plato "was in general suspicious of all bodily appetites" and placed them beneath spirit and reason in the soul [17]. Furthermore, Finnis's claim that Plato found *any* type of sex "'shameful, depraved, and depraving'" is a stretch from simply deeming sex inferior to rational and spiritual activities [18]. Through such crackling debate, Plato breathed new life into the courtroom, influencing major judicial decisions in the recent past.

Platonism after Plato

Plato's ideas caused a stir even in his lifetime. Aristotle famously rebelled against his tutor, finding a different path to eudaemonia and expanding his study to biology, physics, and poetics, among other disciplines. In the Middle Ages, St. Augustine mixed Platonism with

Christianity for a potent path to God–from whom the Forms come, he said [19].

Western philosophy hinged on Plato and his associates. Without him, the Socratic Method would be an obscurity and reason itself might not be seen as the best way to truth.

Still used by teachers to get meaningful responses from students, the systematic inquiry found in the Socratic Method allows true discovery that more deeply engages people in a learning environment. Finding out something for yourself is much more valuable than having it lectured to you, which both Socrates and Plato recognized. And while not everyone agrees that reason matters more than emotion or intuition, for better or for worse, the world still seems to prefer a ratiocentric approach. Almost everything Plato tossed at us has stuck, 2,500 years on.

After the Middle Ages, Plato and his unsparing inquiry formed a driving force behind Renaissance humanism and the Scientific Revolution [20]. Greek Neoplatonic philosopher George Gemithos Plethon, mentioned in Chapter 2 for going against the grain and endorsing Plato in a society that then preferred Aristotle, popularized Plato with the Florentines who had limited access to his works. And they ate it up. His treatise "On the Difference between Aristotle and Plato" brought readers' eyes back to the latter figure after overlooking him. He even worked with Cosimo de' Medici to build the Platonic Academy of Florence [21].

But out of all the gargantuan achievements attributed to Plato during and after his lifetime, his interest in truth may be his greatest legacy. In the "Apology," truth set up tension between Socrates, the sole person *telling* the truth, and the falseness of the many who brought charges against him. In the "Allegory of the Sun," the Forms, Plato claimed, allowed us to see the truth. Today, truth seems more subjective than objective in popular use, with people even referring to telling *their* truth, but plenty still channel Plato in their belief in objective, unchanging truth. Two plus two equals four, after all: no matter if some people disagree. Being founded in sound reason, Plato's truth and pursuit of truth are as accessible today as they were in the ancient world, and he, therefore, keeps inspiring many of us also in pursuit of truth, changing the way we consider the world and our role in it.

Plato almost makes this look easy, but research indicates that pursuing truth is not intuitive. A 2009 meta-analysis of studies with almost 8,000 collective participants relating to congeniality bias, or information that confirms what we already believe, found that the defense motivations for such behavior included "commitment, reversibility, value relevance, quality of available information, confidence, challenge/support, [and] closemindedness," while accuracy motivations included "outcome relevance [and] utility of the available information" [22]. It seems that a greater variety of factors goes into justifying or defending belief than simply aiming to stick to the facts, explaining the smaller list for accuracy motivation. People vacillate between these motivations when exhibiting congeniality bias, especially if it conflicts with a more objective source they might be trying to drown out.

Across the 91 studies, most participants were asked to report an opinion or attitude about an event the researchers brought up. Researchers offered participants information on the event, allowing them to decide, judging by article titles or abstracts, to consume information either corroborating their view or dissenting from it. Half of the information corroborated, and half dissented from participants' views [23].

Careful review of the studies revealed an even more dramatic number: Participants took the congenial route two times more often due to "pre-existing attitudes, beliefs, and behaviors," the meta-analysis concluded, noting that various defense motivations led by a lack of confidence in a less-supported perspective contributed to this congeniality bias [24].

Sorting through biases can be difficult, but the faith Plato puts in his readers is inspiring. The more objective we can be, the closer we are to finding truth.

Action Steps

All Truths

Most of us have topics we can't be objective about—not without some serious Platonic discipline. American presidential candidate Vivek Ramaswamy devised 10 perceived truths in twenty minutes [25]. This simple exercise is meant to help you pinpoint and work on those topics, encouraging you to examine understood "truths" and steer closer to objectivity. Grab a pen and a sheet of paper.

1. Without prior reflection, write down three statements you hold as your greatest truths, leaving space between them.
2. Now consider if any of these are disputable. If not, then try writing down several more.
3. Write your disputes below the disputable statements.
4. Reform any disputable statement into an objective truth. (Using an example from Ramaswamy's list: "There are two genders" could become "I subscribe to the gender binary") [26].
5. Repeat this step until your paper is full of actual truths.

It's okay to be subjective. Holding things dear is part of being human. But being aware of your subjectivity makes it easier to curb such a tendency when you need to be objective about something. After all, sound reasoning leads to truth.

Himself searching for this truth, Plato made early leaps in systematic and political philosophy as well as metaphysics, epistemology, and ethics in his enduring dialogues. He gave us a pathway to knowledge using the Socratic

Method, and if indeed Western philosophy is a footnote to Plato, as Whitehead stated, then we are the better for it. Incorporating Plato's reasoning habits over our appetites and beliefs is not easy but it makes us better thinkers: a worthy reward.

Chapter Summary

- Platonism is a system built on ethics, metaphysics, and epistemology known for using dialogue to discover the truth.
- Questioning and reasoning led Plato and Socrates to the Theory of Forms.
- Plato developed political philosophy with the "Republic," a fundamental text discussing government at length.
- Interpretations of Plato still occur in judicial settings.
- Knowledge of the Forms leads us to truth according to Plato.

CONCLUSION: THE PHILOSOPHER'S GIFT

REVIEW PLATO'S LIFE AND WORK AS COVERED IN THIS BOOK

After being judged in the Myth of Er, the dead lived for a thousand years in heaven or beneath the earth before returning to drink from the River of Forgetfulness. But Er did not drink, instead choosing to remember his journey through the afterlife. As you come away from Plato's ideas and this book, do your best, like Er, to recall your journey here.

Welcoming Plato into your routine is an impactful way to improve your critical thinking, especially using the self-help strategies outlined in past chapters. You can now use what you know about Plato's life–and how it influenced his work–to draw your own conclusions about his work, with the hope that delving deeper into his better-known dialogues will sharpen your philosophical insight into the concepts presented and beyond.

In sum

Plato can be read thematically and/or logically, focusing on either content or biographical and historical context. What we know is compelling. He was tutored by Socrates and courted a potential political career in the early days, witnessing Athens' defeat and fall to tyranny in the Peloponnesian War (which likely influenced the "Republic").

In 399 B.C.E., Socrates stood trial for corrupting the youth of Athens, where he insisted that the Delphic oracle told him he was the wisest man living (see the "Apology"). Although he was executed, Plato preserved his Socratic Method, a dialectical process of reasoning that relied on students discovering philosophical principles for themselves.

At Socrates' deathbed in the "Phaedo," the discussion turned to Forms: invisible, unchanging ideals with concrete iterations in the physical realm. As Forms are unchanging, they are understood as more real than particulars.

The "Parmenides" dialogue contained a discussion between pluralist Socrates and monists Parmenides and Zeno about what is and isn't knowable. Parmenides sensibly asserted that humans can only understand the physical realm, while Socrates argued that true knowledge only existed around Forms.

Forms also factored in the "Allegory of the Cave" in the "Republic," with Plato painting a picture of individuals chained to the side of the cave watching shadows on the wall cast by items outside the cave. Some got the opportunity to leave and see the real world outside, although not without the struggle and growth that comes with education. Plato identified us as the cave dwellers and the real things outside as the Forms invisible to those who couldn't reason.

Leading with reason was a key trait of Plato's philosopher king, introduced earlier in the "Republic." The ruling class needed to be wise, while the military demonstrated courage, and the producers showed temperance, with temperance affecting the other virtues. Together these social classes ran a city, and, when properly executed, the accompanying three cardinal virtues were joined by a fourth: justice. The three virtues also appeared in the human soul, where reason reigned again.

Elsewhere in the "Republic," Plato identified aristocracy as the best form of government, with timocracy, oligarchy, democracy, and tyranny being progressively worse forms of running a state. He also introduced the "Analogy of the Sun" and "Analogy of the Divided Line" to bulk up his case for Forms.

All in all, Platonism is a systematic philosophy based on ethics, metaphysics, and epistemology, in which reason and continued inquiry uncover truth. Plato also pioneered political philosophy with the "Republic" and other works. People continue to interpret him in court and life.

Your own interpretation is valuable, especially now that you have the knowledge base. Take a few minutes to digest ideas, but then get out of your head and discuss what you learned here with someone else, similar to the exercise in [Chapter 9](). See if the two (or more) of you can hatch an original idea. According to dialectical principle, new life begins the second someone else starts talking.

YOUR LAST CHANCE FOR OUR LIMITED DEAL

DID YOU LIKE WHAT YOU READ? THEN YOU'RE GOING TO LOVE THE FOLLOWING EXCLUSIVE OFFER...

In general, around 50% of the people who start reading do not finish a book. You are the exception, and we are happy you took the time.

To honor this, we invite you to join our exclusive Wisdom University newsletter. You cannot find this subscription link anywhere else on the web but in our books!

Upon signing up, you'll receive two of our most popular bestselling books, highly acclaimed by readers like yourself. We sell copies of these books daily, but you will receive them as a gift. Additionally, you'll gain access to two transformative short sheets and enjoy complimentary access to all our upcoming e-books, completely free of charge!

This offer and our newsletter are free; you can unsubscribe anytime.

Here's everything you get:

- ✓ How To Train Your Thinking eBook   ($9.99 Value)
- ✓ The Art Of Game Theory eBook   ($9.99 Value)
- ✓ Break Your Thinking Patterns Sheet   ($4.99 Value)
- ✓ Flex Your Wisdom Muscle Sheet   ($4.99 Value)
- ✓ All our upcoming eBooks   ($199.80* Value)

Total Value: $229.76

Take me to wisdom-university.net for my free bonuses!

(Or simply scan the code with your camera)

Scan Me

*If you download 20 of our books for free, this would equal a value of 199.80$

THE PEOPLE BEHIND WISDOM UNIVERSITY

Michael Meisner, Founder and CEO

When Michael ventured into publishing books on Amazon, he discovered that his favorite topics - the intricacies of the human mind and behavior - were often tackled in a way that's too complex and unengaging. Thus, he dedicated himself to making his ideal a reality: books that effortlessly inform, entertain, and resonate with readers' everyday experiences, enabling them to enact enduring positive changes in their lives.

Together with like-minded people, this ideal became his passion and profession. Michael is in charge of steering the strategic direction and brand orientation of Wisdom University, as he continues to improve and extend his business.

Claire M. Umali, Publishing Manager

Collaborative work lies at the heart of crafting books, and keeping everyone on the same page is an essential task. Claire oversees all the stages of this collaboration, from researching to outlining and from writing to editing. In her free time, she writes online reviews and likes to bother her cats.

Zoe Grabow, Writer

Zoe is an aspiring novelist who has published/presented three papers in philosophy and literature, her favorite era for both being Ancient Greece. With a BA in creative writing and philosophy and a knack for poetry, she enjoys historical fiction, fantasy, film noir, and anything that pushes the bounds of the imagination.

Andrew Speno, Content Editor

Andrew is a teacher, writer, and editor. He has published two historical nonfiction books for middle-grade readers, a biography of Eddie Rickenbacker and the story of the 1928 Bunion Derby ultra-marathon. He enjoys cooking, attending live theater, and playing the ancient game of go.

Sandra Agarrat, Language Editor

Sandra Wall Agarrat is an experienced freelance academic editor/proofreader, writer, and researcher. Sandra holds graduate degrees in Public Policy and International Relations. Her portfolio of projects includes books, dissertations, theses, scholarly articles, and grant proposals.

Mariah B. Girouard, Researcher

Mariah conducts careful research and creates thorough outlines that serve as the basis for Wisdom University's books. She is also a stand-up comedian, spoken word artist, tour guide, and travel writer. Mariah's passion for the arts and the world informs her work and what she produces for Wisdom University.

Ralph Escarda, Layout Designer

Ralph's love for books prevails in his artistic preoccupations. He is an avid reader of non-fictional books and an advocate of self-improvement through education. He dedicates his spare time to doing portraits and sports.

Alpia Villacorta, Layout Designer

Alpia makes sure that each book follows Wisdom University's formatting and design standards, helping it look outstanding, organized, and reader-friendly. She also helps curate suitable images for book covers. For Alpia, becoming an expert layout designer requires a lot of creativity and attention to detail. She believes that maintaining a positive and joyful attitude, along with reading self-help books, can aid in taking care of one's mental health.

Natalie Briggs, Copywriter

Natalie Briggs is a 20-year veteran of the Caribbean's mediascape, having worked as a journalist, editor, broadcaster, and producer in three countries. In 2020, she turned her hand to copywriting and has worked with Wisdom University for two of those three years. She is a graduate of the University of the West Indies and the University of Leicester. She holds a BA in History and Literature and an MA in PR and Communications.

Jemarie Gumban, Hiring Manager

Jemarie is in charge of thoroughly examining and evaluating the profiles and potential of the many aspiring writers and associates for Wisdom University. With an academic background in Applied Linguistics and a meaningful experience as an industrial worker, she approaches her work with a discerning eye and fresh outlook. Guided by her unique perspective, Jemarie derives fulfillment from turning a writer's desire to create motivational literature into tangible reality.

Evangeline Obiedo, Publishing Assistant

Evangeline diligently supports our books' journey, from the writing stage to connecting with our readers. Her commitment to detail permeates her work, encompassing tasks such as initiating profile evaluations and ensuring seamless delivery of our newsletters. Her love for learning extends into the real world - she loves traveling and experiencing new places and cultures.

REFERENCES

Introduction: Experience Growth Mindset

1. Goodreads. (n.d.). *Plato > Quotes > Quotable quote*. Retrieved October 7, 2023, from https://www.goodreads.com/quotes/19198-we-can-easily-forgive-a-child-who-is-afraid-of
2. Rhew, E., Piro, J. S., Goolkasian, P., & Cosentino, P. (2018). The effects of a growth mindset on self-efficacy and motivation. *Cogent Education 5*(1), 1-16, 1-6. https://doi.org/10.1080/2331186X.2018.1492337

1. Navigating Plato

1. Columbia College. (n.d.). *Historical context for Plato*. Columbia College. Retrieved August 23, 2023, from https://www.college.columbia.edu/core/content/republic/context
2. Kim, Y. S. G. (2023). Executive functions and morphological awareness explain the shared variance between word reading and listening comprehension. *Scientific Studies of Reading, 27*(5), 451-474, 451. https://doi.org/10.1080/10888438.2023.2195112
3. Ibid, 456.
4. Kim, Y. S. G. (2020). Toward integrative reading science: The direct and indirect effects model of reading. *Journal of Learning Disabilities, 53*(6), 469-491, 469. https://doi.org/10.1177/0022219420908239
5. Kim, Y. S. G. (2023). Executive functions and morphological awareness explain the shared variance between word reading and listening comprehension. *Scientific Studies of Reading, 27*(5), 451-474, 456-458. https://doi.org/10.1080/10888438.2023.2195112
6. Ibid, 462.
7. He, Y., Liu, X., Hu, J., Nichols, E. S., Lu, C., & Lu, L. (2022). Difference between children and adults in the print-speech coactivated network. *Scientific Studies of Reading, 26*(3), 250-265, 252-262. https://www.tandfonline.com/doi/full/10.1080/10888438.2021.1965607

8. Ikemoto, S. (2008). Dopamine reward circuitry: Two projection systems from the ventral midbrain to the nucleus accumbens-olfactory tubercle complex. *Brain Res Rev 56*(1), 27-78, 27. https://www.ncbi.nlm.nih.gov/pmc/articles/PMC2134972/
   Ventral tegmental area. (2023, August 1). In *Wikipedia*. https://en.wikipedia.org/w/index.php?title=Ventral_tegmental_area&oldid=1168173365
9. Hedges, V. (n.d.). *Brain anatomy*. Michigan State University Libraries. Retrieved August 30, 2023, from https://openbooks.lib.msu.edu/introneuroscience1/chapter/external-brain-anatomy/
10. Ibid.
11. Frede, D. & Lee, M.-K. (2023, February 1). *Plato's ethics: An overview*. Stanford Encyclopedia of Philosophy. https://plato.stanford.edu/entries/plato-ethics/
12. Republic (Plato). (2023, 27 August). In *Wikipedia*. https://en.wikipedia.org/w/index.php?title=Republic_(Plato)&oldid=1172497570
    Brandwood, L. (1990). *The chronology of Plato's dialogues*. Cambridge University Press, 251.

2. Youth, War, And Socratic Influence

1. Plato. (1997). Introduction. In J. M. Cooper (Ed.), *Plato: Complete works* (p. vii). Hackett Publishing Company. https://books.google.com/books?id=fMhgDwAAQBAJ&printsec=frontcover#v=onepage&q&f=false
2. Plato. (n.d.). *Laches*, 196c-d (W. R. M. Lamb, Trans.). *The Perseus Catalog*. https://www.perseus.tufts.edu/hopper/text?doc=Perseus%3Atext%3A1999.01.0176%3Atext%3DLach.%3Asection%3D196c
3. Shakespeare, W. (n.d.) *Julius Caesar*. In B. Mowat, P. Werstine, M. Poston, and R. Niles (Eds.), 77. The Folger Shakespeare. https://www.folger.edu/explore/shakespeares-works/julius-caesar/read/2/2/
4. Plato. (399 B.C.E.). *Crito*, 47e (H. N. Fowler, Trans.). *The Perseus Catalog*. https://www.perseus.tufts.edu/hopper/text?doc=Perseus%3Atext%3A1999.01.0170%3Atext%3DCrito%3Asection%3D47e
5. History.com Editors. (2023, July 7). *Classical Greece*. https://www.history.com/topics/ancient-greece/classical-greece
6. Taylor, A. E. (1926). The Life of Plato. *Plato: The Man and His Work*. Routledge, 1-2.
7. Ibid.

8. Biography.com. (9 August 2023). *Plato*. https://www.biography.com/scholars-educators/plato
9. Pausanias. (1898). *Pausanias's description of Greece*. (J. G. Frazer, Trans.), 138. MacMillan and Co. https://books.google.com/books?id=VqcNAAAAIAAJ&pg=PA138#v=onepage&q&f=false

    First Peloponnesian War. (2023, February 25). In *Wikipedia*. https://en.wikipedia.org/w/index.php?title=First_Peloponnesian_War&oldid=1141568910
10. The Editors of Encyclopaedia Britannica. (n.d.). *Peloponnesian War*. Retrieved July 20, 2023, from https://www.britannica.com/event/Peloponnesian-War
11. Ibid.
12. History.com Editors. (2009). *Peloponnesian War*. https://www.history.com/topics/ancient-greece/peloponnesian-war
13. Biography.com. (9 August 2023). Plato. https://www.biography.com/scholars-educators/plato
14. Meiggs, R. (n.d.). *Alcibiades*. Encyclopedia Britannica. Retrieved July 20, 2023, from https://www.britannica.com/biography/Alcibiades-Athenian-politician-and-general
15. Cartwright, M. (2013, February 8). *Alcibiades*. World History Encyclopedia. https://www.worldhistory.org/Alcibiades/
16. Ibid.
17. The Editors of Encyclopaedia Britannica. (n.d.). *Peloponnesian War*. Encyclopedia Britannica. Retrieved July 20, 2023, from https://www.britannica.com/event/Peloponnesian-War

    Taylor, A. E. (1926). The Life of Plato. *Plato: The man and his work*. Routledge, 1.
18. Planeaux, C. (2015, November 13). *The Thirty Tyrants*. World History Encyclopedia. https://www.worldhistory.org/The_Thirty_Tyrants/
19. Cartledge, P. (1987). *Agesilaos and the crisis of Sparta*, 283. Duckworth. https://books.google.com/books?id=qzJoAAAAMAAJ&focus=searchwithinvolume&q=phyle
20. Planeaux, C. (2015, November 13). *The Thirty Tyrants*. World History Encyclopedia. https://www.worldhistory.org/The_Thirty_Tyrants/
21. Taylor, A. E. (1926). The Life of Plato. *Plato: The man and his work*. Routledge, 3.
22. Ibid, 4.
23. Taylor, A. E. (1926). The Life of Plato. *Plato: The man and his work*. Routledge, 4. The Editors of Encyclopaedia Britannica. (n.d.). *Academy*. Retrieved August 22, 2023, from https://www.britannica.com/topic/Academy-ancient-academy-Athens-Greece

24. Plato. (375 B.C.E.). *Republic*, 443c-444a (P. Shorey, Trans.). *The Perseus Catalog*. http://www.perseus.tufts.edu/hopper/text.jsp?doc=Perseus%3Atext%3A1999.01.0168%3Abook%3D4%3Asection%3D443e
25. Adams, J. P. (2009, May 28). *Platonic chronology and writings*. CSUN.edu. https://www.csun.edu/~hcfll004/platochron.html
26. K.H.O. (2008, October 28). *Parallels between Ray Bradbury's Fahrenheit 451 and Plato's "Allegory of the Cave."* Hana Kiri Writing Portfolio. https://web.archive.org/web/20190606174327/https://www.freewebs.com/hanakiri/WritingPortfolio/essays/Parallels%20between%20Ray%20Bradburys%20Fahrenheit%20451%20and%20Platos%20Allegory%20of%20the%20Cave.htm

    Bradbury, Ray. (1953). *Fahrenheit 451*. The Random House Publishing Group, 139.
27. Plato. (375 B.C.E.). *Republic*, 514a-515a (P. Shorey, Trans.). *The Perseus Catalog*. http://www.perseus.tufts.edu/hopper/text.jsp?doc=Plat.+Rep.+514a&fromdoc=Perseus%3Atext%3A1999.01.0168
28. Ibid, 516b.
29. Campbell-Meikeljohn, D. K., Bach, D. R., Roepstorff, A., & Dolan, R. J. (2010). How the opinion of others affects our valuation of objects. *Current Biology 20*(13), 1165-1170, 1165-6. https://doi.org/10.1016/j.cub.2010.04.055
30. Ibid, 1165-8.

3. The Trial

1. Plato. (n.d.). *Phaedo*, 116d (H. N. Fowler, Trans.). *The Perseus Catalog*. https://www.perseus.tufts.edu/hopper/text?doc=Perseus%3Atext%3A1999.01.0170%3Atext%3DPhaedo%3Asection%3D116d
2. The Editors of Encyclopaedia Britannica. (2023). *Phaedo*. Retrieved July 20, 2023, from https://www.britannica.com/biography/Phaedo-Greek-philosopher
3. Plato. (n.d.). *Phaedo*, 117c (H. N. Fowler, Trans.). *The Perseus Catalog*. https://www.perseus.tufts.edu/hopper/text?doc=Plat.+Phaedo+117c&fromdoc=Perseus%3Atext%3A1999.01.0170
4. Tetrault, S. (2022, Sept. 1). *Why Professional Mourners Exist And What They Actually Do*. Cake. https://www.joincake.com/blog/professional-mourners/
5. Mund, M., & Mitte, K. (2012). The costs of repression: a meta-analysis on the relation between repressive coping and somatic

diseases, *Health Psychology 31*(5), 640-649, 640.https://doi.org/10.1037/a0026257
6. Ibid, 641-643.
7. Ibid, 645.
8. Ibid.
9. Plato. (399 B.C.E.). *Apology*, 17c (H. N. Fowler, Trans.). *The Perseus Catalog.* https://www.perseus.tufts.edu/hopper/text?doc=Perseus%3Atext%3A1999.01.0170%3Atext%3DApol.%3Asection%3D17c
10. Plato. (n.d.). *Phaedo*, 75b (H. N. Fowler, Trans.). *The Perseus Catalog.* https://www.perseus.tufts.edu/hopper/text?doc=Plat.+Phaedo+75b&fromdoc=Perseus%3Atext%3A1999.01.0170
11. Plato. (375 B.C.E.). *Republic*, 340d (P. Shorey, Trans.). *The Perseus Catalog.* http://www.perseus.tufts.edu/hopper/text.jsp?doc=Plat.+Rep.+340d&fromdoc=Perseus%3Atext%3A1999.01.0168
12. Kraut, R. (n.d.). *Socrates*. Encyclopedia Britannica. Retrieved July 20, 2023, from https://www.britannica.com/biography/Socrates
13. Ibid.
14. King, I. (2014, January 15). *Thinkers at war - Socrates*. Military History Matters. https://www.military-history.org/feature/thinkers-at-war-socrates.htm
15. Ibid.
16. Ibid.
17. Kraut, R. (n.d.). *Socrates*. Encyclopedia Britannica. Retrieved July 20, 2023, from https://www.britannica.com/biography/Socrates
18. Ibid.
19. Meinwald, C. (2023, June 16). *Plato*. Encyclopedia Britannica. https://www.britannica.com/biography/Plato
20. Taplin, O., & Woodard, T. M. (2023, Sep 21). *Sophocles*. Encyclopedia Britannica. https://www.britannica.com/biography/Sophocles
21. Plato. (399 B.C.E.). *Apology*, 17a (H. N. Fowler, Trans.). *The Perseus Catalog.* https://www.perseus.tufts.edu/hopper/text?doc=Perseus%3Atext%3A1999.01.0170%3Atext%3DApol.%3Asection%3D17a
22. Ibid, 19b.
23. Xenophon. (n.d.) *Hellenica*, 36. *The Perseus Catalog.* http://www.perseus.tufts.edu/hopper/text?doc=Xen.+Hell.+2.4.&fromdoc=Perseus%3Atext%3A1999.01.0206
24. Plato. (399 B.C.E.). *Apology*, 24c (H. N. Fowler, Trans.). *The Perseus Catalog.* https://www.perseus.tufts.edu/hopper/text?doc=Plat.+Apol.+24c&fromdoc=Perseus%3Atext%3A1999.01.0170
25. Ibid, 21a.
26. Ibid, 21e.
27. Ibid, 23b.

28. Ibid, 23c.
29. Ibid, 24d.
30. Ibid, 27e.
31. Ibid, 28a.
32. Ibid, 28c-d.
33. Ibid, 29a.
34. Ibid, 29d.
35. Ibid, 30e.
36. Ibid, 36a.
37. Ibid, 37d.
38. Ibid, 41e.
39. Plato. (353 B.C.E.). *Letters,* 324d-e (R. G. Bury, Trans.). *The Perseus Catalog.* https://www.perseus.tufts.edu/hopper/text?doc=Perseus:text:1999.01.0164:letter=7
40. Ibid, 324e-325a.
41. Ibid, 325a-c.
42. Kraut, R. (n.d.). *Socrates.* Encyclopedia Britannica. Retrieved July 20, 2023, from https://www.britannica.com/biography/Socrates
43. Ferguson, J., & Balsdon, J. P. V. D. (2023). *Cicero.* Encyclopedia Britannica. https://www.britannica.com/biography/Cicero
44. Aguiar, O. G., Mortimer, E. F., & Scott, P. (2010). Learning from and responding to students' questions: The authoritative and dialogic tension. *Journal of Research in Science Teaching 47*(2), 174-193. https://doi.org/10.1002/tea.20315
45. Ibid, 178.
46. Ibid, 181-2.
47. Ibid, 182-5.
48. Ibid, 185-7.
49. Ibid, 187-8.
50. Ibid, 188-9.

4. Distant Ideals No More

1. Plato. (384 B.C.E.). *Euthydemus,* 291c. (W.R.M. Lamb, Trans.). *The Perseus Catalog.* https://www.perseus.tufts.edu/hopper/text?doc=Perseus%3Atext%3A1999.01.0178%3Atext%3DEuthyd.%3Asection%3D291c
2. Plato. (399 B.C.E.). *Crito,* 44b-45c (H. N. Fowler, Trans.). *The Perseus Catalog.* https://www.perseus.tufts.edu/hopper/text?doc=Plat.+Crito+44b&fromdoc=Perseus%3Atext%3A1999.01.0170
3. Plato, *Crito,* 47c.

4. Adams, J. P. (2009, May 28). *Platonic chronology and writings*. CSUN.edu. https://www.csun.edu/~hcfll004/platochron.html
5. Plato. (1997). Introduction. In J. M. Cooper (Ed.), *Plato: Complete works* (p. xiv). Hackett Publishing Company. https://books.google.com/books?id=fMhgDwAAQBAJ&printsec=frontcover#v=onepage&q&f=false
6. Plato. (399 B.C.E.). *Crito*, 48c (H. N. Fowler, Trans.). *The Perseus Catalog*. https://www.perseus.tufts.edu/hopper/text?doc=Plat.+Crito+48c&fromdoc=Perseus%3Atext%3A1999.01.0170
7. Hale, B. (n.d.). *Realism*. Encyclopedia Britannica. Retrieved July 20, 2023, from https://www.britannica.com/topic/realism-philosophy
8. Plato. (n.d.). *Phaedo*, 57a-58d (H. N. Fowler, Trans.). *The Perseus Catalog*. https://www.perseus.tufts.edu/hopper/text?doc=Plat.+Phaedo+57a&fromdoc=Perseus%3Atext%3A1999.01.0170
9. Ibid, 64c.
10. Ibid, 64e.
11. Ibid, 65b.
12. Ibid, 66c-67b.
13. Ibid, 67e.
14. Ibid, 70a.
15. Ibid, 70c.
16. Ibid, 71e.
17. Ibid, 72b-c.
18. Ibid, 73c.
19. Ibid, 74a.
20. Ibid, 75a.
21. Ibid.
22. Ibid, 75c.
23. Ibid, 75e.
24. Ibid, 76c.
25. Merriam-Webster. (n.d.). Affinity. Retrieved August 29, 2023, from https://www.merriam-webster.com/dictionary/affinity
26. Plato. (n.d.). *Phaedo*, 79b-c (H. N. Fowler, Trans.). *The Perseus Catalog*. https://www.perseus.tufts.edu/hopper/text?doc=Plat.+Phaedo+79b&fromdoc=Perseus%3Atext%3A1999.01.0170
27. Ibid, 78e.
28. Ibid, 79a-b.
29. Ibid, 83d-e.
30. Ibid, 85e.
31. Ibid, 86a-b.
32. Ibid, 85e-86d.
33. Ibid, 87c-88b.
34. Ibid, 92b-c.

35. Ibid, 94c-d.
36. Lanza, R. (2011, December 21). Does the soul exist? Evidence says 'Yes.' *Psychology Today*. https://www.psychologytoday.com/us/blog/biocentrism/201112/does-the-soul-exist-evidence-says-yes
37. Mann, A. (2020, February 28). Schrödinger's Cat: The favorite, misunderstood pet of quantum mechanics. *Live Science*. https://www.livescience.com/schrodingers-cat.html
38. Gerlich, S., Eibenberger, S., Tomandl, M. Nimmrichter, S., Hornberger, K., Fagan, P. J., Tüxen, J., Mayor, M., & Arndt, M. (2011, April 5). Quantum interference of large organic molecules. *Nature Communications* 2, 1-5, 1. https://doi.org/10.1038/ncomms1263
39. Merriam-Webster. (n.d.). Interferometer. In *Merriam-Webster.com* dictionary. Retrieved August 29, 2023, from https://www.merriam-webster.com/dictionary/interferometer
40. Gerlich, S., Eibenberger, S., Tomandl, M. Nimmrichter, S., Hornberger, K., Fagan, P. J., Tüxen, J., Mayor, M., & Arndt, M. (2011, April 5). Quantum interference of large organic molecules. *Nature Communications* 2, 1-5, 2. https://doi.org/10.1038/ncomms1263
41. Ibid, 4.
42. Lanza, R. (2011, December 21). Does the soul exist? Evidence says 'Yes.' *Psychology Today*. https://www.psychologytoday.com/us/blog/biocentrism/201112/does-the-soul-exist-evidence-says-yes
43. Ibid.
44. Ibid.
45. Locke, E.A., Shaw, K. N., Saari, L. M., & Latham, G. P. (1981). Goal setting and task performance: 1969-1980. *Psychological Bulletin*, *90*(1), 125-152, 129. https://doi.org/10.1037/0033-2909.90.1.125
46. Doran, G. T. (1981, November). There's a S.M.A.R.T. way to write management's goals and objectives. *AMA Forum*, 35-36. https://community.mis.temple.edu/mis0855002fall2015/files/2015/10/S.M.A.R.T-Way-Management-Review.pdf
47. Cherry, K. (2022, December 16). Piaget's 4 stages of cognitive development explained. *Verywell Mind*. https://www.verywellmind.com/piagets-stages-of-cognitive-development-2795457

5. Parmenides Versus Plato

1. Plato. *Parmenides*, 128a (H. N. Fowler, Trans.). *The Perseus Catalog*. https://www.perseus.tufts.edu/hopper/text?doc=Perseus%3Atext%

3A1999.01.0174%3Atext%3DParm.%3Asection%3D128a
2. Hugget, N. (2018, June 11). *Zeno's paradoxes*. Stanford Encyclopedia of Philosophy. https://plato.stanford.edu/entries/paradox-zeno/#Arr
3. Parmenides (dialogue). (2023, September 3). In *Wikipedia*. https://en.wikipedia.org/w/index.php?title= Parmenides_(dialogue)&oldid=1173629165

    Rickless, S. (2020, January 14). *Plato's Parmenides*. Stanford Encyclopedia of Philosophy. https://plato.stanford.edu/archives/spr2020/entries/plato-parmenides/
4. Plato. *Parmenides*, 135c (H. N. Fowler, Trans.). *The Perseus Catalog*. https://www.perseus.tufts.edu/hopper/text?doc=Plat.+Parm.+135c&fromdoc=Perseus%3Atext%3A1999.01.0174
5. Ibid, 127b.
6. Ibid, 127c.
7. Rickless, S. (2020, January 14). *Plato's Parmenides*. Stanford Encyclopedia of Philosophy. https://plato.stanford.edu/archives/spr2020/entries/plato-parmenides/
8. Parmenides *(dialogue)*. *(2023, September 3). In Wikipedia. https://en.wikipedia.org/w/index.php?title= Parmenides_(dialogue)&oldid=1173629165*

    Plato. *Parmenides*, 133a (H. N. Fowler, Trans.). *The Perseus Catalog*. https://www.perseus.tufts.edu/hopper/text?doc=Plat.+Parm.+133a&fromdoc=Perseus%3Atext%3A1999.01.0174
9. Ibid, 135c.
10. Ibid, 135d.
11. Ibid, 135e-136a.
12. Ibid, 127e.
13. Plato. *Parmenides*, 129d-130a (H. N. Fowler, Trans.). *The Perseus Catalog*. https://www.perseus.tufts.edu/hopper/text?doc=Plat.+Parm.+129d&fromdoc=Perseus%3Atext%3A1999.01.0174

    Parmenides (dialogue). (2023, September 3). In *Wikipedia*. *https://en.wikipedia.org/w/index.php?title= Parmenides_(dialogue)&oldid=1173629165*
14. Plato. *Parmenides*, 127e-130a (H. N. Fowler, Trans.). *The Perseus Catalog*. https://www.perseus.tufts.edu/hopper/text?doc=Plat.+Parm.+127e&fromdoc=Perseus%3Atext%3A1999.01.0174
15. Ibid, 131c.
16. Ibid, 131b.
17. Ibid, 131b-c.
18. Ibid, 132a.
19. Ibid, 132a-b.
20. Ibid.

21. Ibid.
22. Ibid, 133d-134a.
23. Parmenides (dialogue). (2023, September 3). In *Wikipedia*. https://en.wikipedia.org/w/index.php?title=Parmenides_(dialogue)&oldid=1173629165
    Plato. *Parmenides*, 134a-c (H. N. Fowler, Trans.). *The Perseus Catalog*. https://www.perseus.tufts.edu/hopper/text?doc=Plat.+Parm.+134a&fromdoc=Perseus%3Atext%3A1999.01.0174
24. Plato. *Parmenides*, 137c-d (H. N. Fowler, Trans.). *The Perseus Catalog*. https://www.perseus.tufts.edu/hopper/text?doc=Plat.+Parm.+137c&fromdoc=Perseus%3Atext%3A1999.01.0174
25. Ibid, 137d.
26. Ibid, 137d-138a.
27. Ibid, 138a.
28. Ibid, 138a-138b.
29. Ibid, 138b-139b.
30. Parmenides (dialogue). (2023, September 3). In *Wikipedia*. https://en.wikipedia.org/w/index.php?title=Parmenides_(dialogue)&oldid=1173629165
    Plato. *Parmenides*, 142c (H. N. Fowler, Trans.). *The Perseus Catalog*. https://www.perseus.tufts.edu/hopper/text?doc=Plat.+Parm.+142c&fromdoc=Perseus%3Atext%3A1999.01.0174
31. Plato. *Parmenides*, 142c-d (H. N. Fowler, Trans.). *The Perseus Catalog*. https://www.perseus.tufts.edu/hopper/text?doc=Plat.+Parm.+142c&fromdoc=Perseus%3Atext%3A1999.01.0174
32. Ibid, 153c.
33. Ibid.
34. Ibid, 153d-154b.
35. Ibid, 157b.
36. Ibid, 155e.
37. Ibid, 155e-156c.
38. Ibid, 156c-156d.
39. Ibid, 158e-159a.
40. Porter, T., Elnakouri, A., Meyers, E. A., Shibayama, T., Jayawickreme, E., & Grossman, Igor. (2022). Predictors and consequences of intellectual humility. *Nature Reviews Psychology*, *1*, 524-536. https://doi.org/10.1038/s44159-022-00081-9
41. Grossman, I., Weststrate, N. M., Ardelt, M., Brienza, J., Dong, M., Ferrari, M., Fournier, M. A., Hu, C. S., Nusbaum, H., & Vervacke, J. (2020). The science of wisdom in a polarized world: Knowns and unknowns. *Psychological Inquiry*, *31*(2), 103-133. https://doi.org/10.31234/osf.io/w9ygc

42. Mueller-Bloch, C., & Kranz, J. (2015). A framework for rigorously identifying research gaps in qualitative literature reviews. *Proceedings of the 36th International Conference on Information Systems (ICIS)*, 1-19, 6. https://www.researchgate.net/publication/283271278_A_Framework_for_Rigorously_Identifying_Research_Gaps_in_Qualitative_Literature_Reviews/link/562fd50608aea4ccc6dddb8c/download
43. Ibid, 10.

6. Plato's Famous Cave Allegory

1. Plato. (375 B.C.E.). *Republic*, 514b (P. Shorey, Trans.). *The Perseus Catalog*. http://www.perseus.tufts.edu/hopper/text.jsp?doc=Plat.+Rep.+514b&fromdoc=Perseus%3Atext%3A1999.01.0168
2. Ibid, 514a-515c.
3. Ibid, 515c.
4. Ibid, 514a.
5. Bacon, F. (1620). *Novum organum*, Aphorism LIII. *The Project Gutenberg*. https://www.gutenberg.org/files/45988/45988-h/45988-h.htm
    Allegory of the cave. (2023, September 4). In *Wikipedia*. https://en.wikipedia.org/w/index.php?title=Allegory_of_the_cave&oldid=1173878097
6. Muennig, P., Schweinhart, L., Montie, J., Neidell, M. (2009). Effects of a prekindergarten educational intervention on adult health: 37-year follow-up results of a randomized controlled trial. *Am J Public Health*, 99(8), 1431-1437, 1431. https://doi.org/10.2105/AJPH.2008.148353
7. Plato. (375 B.C.E.). *Republic*, 515b (P. Shorey, Trans.). *The Perseus Catalog*. http://www.perseus.tufts.edu/hopper/text.jsp?doc=Plat.+Rep.+515b&fromdoc=Perseus%3Atext%3A1999.01.0168
8. Ibid, 518d-519b.
9. Ibid, 518c.
10. Ibid.
11. Ibid, 520c.
12. Ibid, 519d
13. Wood, W. & Rünger, D. (2016). Psychology of habit. *Review of Psychology* 67, 289-314, 292. https://doi.org/10.1146/annurev-psych-122414-033417
14. Wood, W. & Rünger, D. (2016). Psychology of habit. *Review of Psychology* 67, 289-314, 305. https://doi.org/10.1146/annurev-psych-122414-033417

Lin, P. Y., Wood, W., & Monterosso, J. (2016). Healthy eating habits protect against temptations. *Appetite*, 432-440, 432. https://doi.org/10.1016/j.appet.2015.11.011

15. Allegory of the cave. (2023, September 4). In *Wikipedia*. https://en.wikipedia.org/w/index.php?title=Allegory_of_the_cave&oldid=1173878097

7. Bask In The Philosopher King's Glory

1. Shea, C. (2012, October). Why power corrupts. *Smithsonian Magazine*. https://www.smithsonianmag.com/science-nature/why-power-corrupts-37165345/
2. DeCelles, K. A., DeRue, D. S., Margolis, J. D., & Ceranic, T. L. (2012). Does power corrupt or enable? When and why power facilitates self-interested behavior. *American Psychological Foundation*, *97*(3), 681-689, 681. http://www.doi.org/10.1037/a0026811
3. Ibid, 683.
4. Ibid.
5. Ibid.
6. Ibid.
7. Shea, C. (2012, October). Why power corrupts. *Smithsonian Magazine*. https://www.smithsonianmag.com/science-nature/why-power-corrupts-37165345/
8. DeCelles, K. A., DeRue, D. S., Margolis, J. D., & Ceranic, T. L. (2012). Does power corrupt or enable? When and why power facilitates self-interested behavior. *American Psychological Foundation*, *97*(3), 681-689, 683. http://www.doi.org/10.1037/a0026811
9. Shea, C. (2012, October). Why power corrupts. *Smithsonian Magazine*. https://www.smithsonianmag.com/science-nature/why-power-corrupts-37165345/
10. DeCelles, K. A., DeRue, D. S., Margolis, J. D., & Ceranic, T. L. (2012). Does power corrupt or enable? When and why power facilitates self-interested behavior. *American Psychological Foundation*, *97*(3), 681-689, 683. http://www.doi.org/10.1037/a0026811
11. Plato. (375 B.C.E.). *Republic*, 515b (P. Shorey, Trans.). *The Perseus Catalog*. http://www.perseus.tufts.edu/hopper/text.jsp?doc=Plat.+Rep.+473d&fromdoc=Perseus%3Atext%3A1999.01.0168
12. Ibid, 414e-415c.
13. Ibid, 428e-429b.
14. Ibid, 431e.
15. Ibid, 428e.

16. Ibid, 412e.
17. Ibid, 416c-e.
18. Ibid, 487c-d.
19. Surowiecki, J. (2004). *The wisdom of crowds.* Anchor Books.
20. Orlitzky, M. (n.d.). *Free market.* Encyclopedia Britannica. Retrieved August 28, 2023, from https://www.britannica.com/money/free market

    Free market. (2023, September 10). In *Wikipedia.* https://en.wikipedia.org/w/index.php?title=Free_market&oldid=1174744696
21. Plato. (375 B.C.E.). *Republic*, 476a (P. Shorey, Trans.). *The Perseus Catalog.* http://www.perseus.tufts.edu/hopper/text.jsp?doc=Plat.+Rep.+476a&fromdoc=Perseus%3Atext%3A1999.01.0168
22. Ibid, 475e.
23. Ibid, 485c.
24. Ibid, 485d-486b.
25. Ibid, 487a.
26. Ibid, 451e-452a.
27. Ibid, 376e-377a.
28. Ibid, 377d.
29. Ibid, 387b.
30. Ibid, 387c-e.
31. Ibid, 389d.
32. Ibid, 390a.
33. Ibid, 433b.
34. Shafir, E., Simonson, I., & Tversky, A. (1993). Reason-based choice. *Cognition, 49*, 11-36, 14. https://doi.org/10.1016/0010-0277(93)90034-s

    Slovic, P. (1975). Choice between equally valued alternatives. *Journal of Experimental Psychology: Human Perception and Performance, 1*(3), 280-287, 280. https://doi.org/10.1037/0096-1523.1.3.280
35. Shafir, E., Simonson, I., & Tversky, A. (1993). Reason-based choice. *Cognition, 49*, 11-36, 14. https://doi.org/10.1016/0010-0277(93)90034-s
36. Ibid.
37. Keating, K., Rosch, D., & Burgoon, L. (2014). Developmental readiness for leadership: The differential effects of leadership courses on creating "ready, willing, and able" leaders. *Journal of Leadership Education*, 1-16, 3. https://journalofleadershiped.org/jole_articles/developmental-readiness-for-leadership-the-differential-effects-of-leadership-courses-on-creating-ready-willing-and-able-leaders/
38. Ibid, 4.
39. Ibid, 6-7.

40. Ibid, 7.
41. Ibid, 11.
42. Plato. (375 B.C.E.). *Republic*. 414d-415d (P. Shorey, Trans.). The Perseus Catalog. http://www.perseus.tufts.edu/hopper/text.jsp?doc=Plat.+Rep.+414d&fromdoc=Perseus%3Atext%3A1999.01.0168
43. Littmann, G. (2016). "The needs of the many outweigh the needs of the few": Utilitarianism and Star Trek. In K. S. Decker & J. T. Ebert (Eds.), *The ultimate Star Trek and philosophy: The search for Socrates*. Wiley Online Library. https://doi.org/10.1002/9781119146032.ch12
44. Lippmann, W. (1922). *Public Opinion*. Harcourt, Brace and Company, 13.
45. Ibid, 202.

8. An Ethical Inquiry

1. Disneyclips. (n.d.). *Give a little whistle*. Retrieved September 1, 2023, from https://www.disneyclips.com/lyrics/lyrics79.html
2. Frede, D., & Lee, M.-K. (2023, February 1). *Plato's ethics: An overview*. Stanford Encyclopedia of Philosophy. https://plato.stanford.edu/entries/plato-ethics/
3. Ibid.
4. Fredrickson, B. L., Grewen, K. M., Coffey, K. A., Algoe, S. B., Firestone, A. M., Arevalo, J. M. G., Ma, J., & Cole, S. W. (2013). A functional genomic perspective on human well-being. *Proceedings of the Natural Academy of Sciences, 110*(33), 13684-9, 13684. https://doi.org/10.1073/pnas.1305419110
5. Ibid.
6. Ibid, 13685.
7. Ibid, 13684.
8. Ibid, 13685.
9. Ibid.
10. Plato. (375 B.C.E.). *Republic*, 359e (P. Shorey, Trans.). *The Perseus Catalog*. http://www.perseus.tufts.edu/hopper/text.jsp?doc=Plat.+Rep.+359e&fromdoc=Perseus%3Atext%3A1999.01.0168
11. Ibid, 360 a-d.
12. Ibid, 353b.
13. Ibid, 353e.
14. Ibid, 427e.
15. Ibid, 428d.

16. Ibid, 428c.
17. Ibid, 429c.
18. Ibid, 430a.
19. Ibid, 432a-b.
20. Ibid, 432a.
21. Aristotle. *Nicomachean Ethics*, 1115a. (H. Rackham, Trans.). *The Perseus Catalog*. https://www.perseus.tufts.edu/hopper/text?doc=Perseus%3Atext%3A1999.01.0054%3Abekker%20page%3D1115a
22. Exum, M. L. (2015). The role of emotion and reason in criminal decision making. *International Journal of Offender Therapy and Comparative Criminology, 59*(13), 1383-4, 1383. https://doi.org/10.1177/0306624X15612718
23. Encyclopedia.com (n.d.). *Expected utility theory*. Retrieved September 1, 2023, from https://www.encyclopedia.com/social-sciences/applied-and-social-sciences-magazines/expected-utility-theory
24. Johnson-Laird, P. N., & Shafir, E. (1993). The interaction between reasoning and decision making: An introduction. *Cognition, 49*, 1-9. https://doi.org/10.1016/0010-0277(93)90033-R

9. The Perfect Society

1. Savage, M., Devine, F., Cunningham, N., Taylor, M., Li, Y., Hjellbrekke, J., Le Roux, B. Friedman, S., & Miles, A. (2013). A new model of social class? Findings from the BBC's Great British Class Survey experiment. *Sociology, 47*(2), 219-250, 220. https://doi.org/10.1177/0038038513481128
2. Ibid, 230.
3. Ibid, 222.
4. Ibid, 230.
5. Ibid, 231.
6. Steinberger, P. J. (1996). Who is Cephalus? *Political Theory, 24*(2), 172-199, 175. https://www.jstor.org/stable/192114
7. Plato. (375 B.C.E.). *Republic*, 330e-331b (P. Shorey, Trans.). *The Perseus Catalog*. http://www.perseus.tufts.edu/hopper/text.jsp?doc=Plat.+Rep.+330e&fromdoc=Perseus%3Atext%3A1999.01.0168
8. Ibid, 358a.
9. Ibid, 368e.
10. Ibid, 427c-434d.
11. Ibid, 424a.
12. Ibid, 492a.
13. Ibid, 488a-489a.

14. Ibid, 582c.
15. Ibid, 614c-d.
16. Ibid, 617d-619c.
17. Ibid, 620d-621d.
18. Ibid, 544c.
19. Ibid, 424a.
20. Merriam-Webster (n.d.). Aristocracy. In *Merriam-Webster.com dictionary*. Retrieved August 17, 2023, from https://www.merriam-webster.com/dictionary/aristocracy
21. Plato. (375 B.C.E.). *Republic*, 330e (P. Shorey, Trans.). *The Perseus Catalog*. http://www.perseus.tufts.edu/hopper/text.jsp?doc=Plat.+Rep.+330e&fromdoc=Perseus%3Atext%3A1999.01.0168
22. Ibid, 546b-d.
23. Ibid, 546d-547a.
24. Ibid, 544c.
25. Ibid, 547d-548b.
26. Ibid, 549c.
27. Ibid, 549c-e.
28. Ibid, 549b-550c.
29. Ibid, 550c-551c.
30. Ibid, 550c-554a.
31. Ibid, 552d-555b.
32. Ibid, 557a.
33. Ibid, 557b-558a.
34. Ibid, 559c-560d.
35. Ibid, 560d-561a.
36. Ibid, 561b-563e.
37. Ibid, 565c.
38. Ibid, 565c-566a.
39. Ibid.
40. Ibid, 566b-566c.
41. Ibid, 566e-569c.
42. Ibid, 353c.
43. Ibid, 344c.
44. Ibid, 345a.
45. Ibid, 346c-347c.
46. Ibid, 359d-e.
47. Ibid, 359d-360d.
48. Ibid, 433b.
49. Ibid, 615a-c.
50. Ibid, 507b-509c.
51. Ibid, 509d-511e.
52. Ibid.

53. Ibid, 509d-511c.
54. Ibid, 511c.
55. Ibid, 510e-511a.
56. Hallowell, J. H. (1965). Plato and his critics. *The Journal of Politics* 27(2), 273-289, 274. https://www.jstor.org/stable/2128073
57. Ibid, 274-7.
58. Trueman, C N. (2015, March 9). *Blood and soil*. History Learning Site. https://www.historylearningsite.co.uk/nazi-germany/blood-and-soil/
59. Plato. (375 B.C.E.). *Republic*, 435c-436a (P. Shorey, Trans.). *The Perseus Catalog*. http://www.perseus.tufts.edu/hopper/text.jsp?doc=Plat.+Rep.+435e&fromdoc=Perseus%3Atext%3A1999.01.0168
60. Ibid, 469b-471c.
61. Bobonich, C. (Ed.). (2017). *The Cambridge companion to ancient ethics*. Cambridge University Press, 298. https://doi.org/10.1017/9781107284258
62. Ibid, 299.
63. Hallowell, J. H. (1965). Plato and his critics. *The Journal of Politics* 27(2), 273-289, 275. https://www.jstor.org/stable/2128073
64. Ibid, 274.
65. Merriam-Webster. (n.d.). Propaganda. In *Merriam-Webster.com dictionary*. Retrieved July 20, 2023, from https://www.merriam-webster.com/dictionary/propaganda
66. Hallowell, J. H. (1965). Plato and his critics. *The Journal of Politics* 27(2), 273-289, 274. https://www.jstor.org/stable/2128073
67. Guerrero, T. A., & Wiley, J. (2021). Expecting to teach affects learning during study of expository texts. *Journal of Educational Psychology, 113*(7), 1281-1303, 1284. https://doi.org/10.1037/edu0000657
68. Ibid, 1283-1291.
69. Terada, Y., Merril, S., & Gonser, S. (2021, December 9). The 10 most significant education studies of 2021. *Edutopia*. https://www.edutopia.org/article/10-most-significant-education-studies-2021
70. Agence France-Presse. (2021, November 22). US added to list of 'backsliding' democracies for first time. *The Guardian*. https://www.theguardian.com/us-news/2021/nov/22/us-list-backsliding-democracies-civil-liberties-international

10. Echoes Of Plato

1. Maroto-Rodriguez, J., Delgado-Velandia, M., Ortolá, R., Perez-Cornago, A., Kales, S. N., Rodriguez-Artalejo, F., & Sotos-Prieto, M. (2023). Association of a Mediterranean lifestyle with all-cause and cause-specific mortality: A prospective study from the UK Biobank. *Mayo Clinic Proceedings.* https://doi.org/10.1016/j.mayocp.2023.05.031
2. Harvard T.H. Chan School of Public Health. (2023, August 16). Adherence to a Mediterranean lifestyle associated with lower risk of all-cause and cancer mortality. *Science Daily.* https://www.sciencedaily.com/releases/2023/08/230816170623.htm
3. Columbia College. (n.d.). *A.N. Whitehead on Plato.* https://www.college.columbia.edu/core/content/whitehead-plato
4. The Editors of Encyclopaedia Britannica. (n.d.). Plato summary. Retrieved August 21, 2013. https://www.britannica.com/summary/Plato
5. Systems philosophy. (2023, June 30). In *Wikipedia.* https://en.wikipedia.org/w/index.php?title=Systems_philosophy&oldid=1162713117
6. Bertalanffy, L. von. (1976). *General system theory.* New York: George Braziller, xi-xiv.
7. Ibid, xxvii.
8. BBC News. (2019, 19 June). What is India's Caste System? *BBC News.* https://www.bbc.com/news/world-asia-india-35650616
9. Ibid.
10. Goodreads. (n.d.). John F. Kennedy > Quotes. Retrieved August 21, 2023, from https://www.goodreads.com/author/quotes/3047.John_F_Kennedy
11. BBC News. (2014, 17 April). *Study: US is an oligarchy, not a democracy.* BBC News. https://www.bbc.com/news/blogs-echochambers-27074746
12. Gilens, M., & Page, B. I. (2014). Testing theories of American politics: Elites, interest groups, and average citizens. *Perspectives on Politics, 12*(3), 564-581, 576. https://doi.org/10.1017/S1537592714001595
13. Wheeler-Bell, Q. (2017). Educating the elite: A social justice education for the privileged class. *Philosophical Inquiry in Education 24*(4), 379-399. https://files.eric.ed.gov/fulltext/EJ1162792.pdf
14. Merriam-Webster (n.d.) Justice. In *Merriam-Webster.com dictionary.* Retrieved August 21, 2023, from https://www.merriam-webster.com/dictionary/justice

15. Carnes, J. (2007). Plato in the Courtroom: The Surprising Influence of the Symposium on Legal Theory. In J. Lesher, D. Nails, F. Sheffield (Eds.), *Plato's Symposium: Issues in interpretation and reception*. Hellenic Studies Series 22. Washington, DC: Center for Hellenic Studies. Retrieved August 21, 2023, from https://chs.harvard.edu/chapter/12-plato-in-the-courtroom-the-surprising influence of the-symposium-on-legal-theory-jeffrey-carnes/
16. Ibid.
17. Ibid.
18. Ibid.
19. Robinson, Nick. (n.d.) *Platonic Influence on St. Augustine's Philosophy*. SeattlePi. Retrieved August 21, 2023, from https://education.seattlepi.com/platonic-influence-st-augustines-philosophy-5566.html
20. Mysterium Academy. (n.d.). *10 ways Plato has influenced the modern world*. Retrieved 21 August 2023, from https://mysteriumacademy.com/10-ways-plato-has-influenced-the-modern-world/#google_vignette
21. The Editors of Encyclopaedia Britannica. (n. d.). *George Gemistus Plethon*. Retrieved on August 21, 2023, from https://www.britannica.com/biography/George-Gemistus-Plethon
22. Hart, W., Albarracin, D., Eagly, A. H., Brechan, I., Lindberg, M. J., & Merrill, L. (2009). Feeling validated versus being correct: A meta-analysis of selective exposure to information. *Psychological Bulletin 135*(4), 555-588, 557-9. https://doi.org/10.1037/a0015701
23. Ibid, 556.
24. Ibid, 579.
25. Gentile, L. (2023, August 18). Ramaswamy praised by conservatives after publishing 10 'truths' on X. *Washington Examiner*. https://www.washingtonexaminer.com/news/ramaswamy-praised-by-conservatives-after-publishing-10-truths-on-x
26. Ibid.

DISCLAIMER

The information contained in this book and its components, is meant to serve as a comprehensive collection of strategies that the author of this book has done research about. Summaries, strategies, tips and tricks are only recommendations by the author, and reading this book will not guarantee that one's results will exactly mirror the author's results.

The author of this book has made all reasonable efforts to provide current and accurate information for the readers of this book. The author and their associates will not be held liable for any unintentional errors or omissions that may be found, and for damages arising from the use or misuse of the information presented in this book.

Readers should exercise their own judgment and discretion in interpreting and applying the information to their specific circumstances. This book is not intended to replace professional advice (especially medical advice, diagnosis, or treatment). Readers are encouraged to seek appropriate professional guidance for their individual needs.

The material in the book may include information by third parties. Third party materials comprise of opinions expressed by their owners. As such, the author of this book does not assume responsibility or liability for any third party material or opinions.

The publication of third party material does not constitute the author's guarantee of any information, products, services, or opinions contained within third party material. Use of third party material does not guarantee that your results will mirror our results. Publication of such third party material is simply a recommendation and expression of the author's own opinion of that material.

Whether because of the progression of the Internet, or the unforeseen changes in company policy and editorial submission guidelines, what is stated as fact at the time of this writing may become outdated or inapplicable later.

Wisdom University is committed to respecting copyright laws and intellectual property rights. We have taken reasonable measures to ensure that all quotes, diagrams, figures, images, tables, and other information used in this publication are either created by us, obtained with permission, or fall under fair use guidelines. However, if any copyright infringement has inadvertently occurred, please notify us promptly at wisdom-university@mail.net, providing sufficient details to identify the specific material in question. We will take immediate action to rectify the situation, which may include obtaining necessary permissions, making corrections, or removing the material in subsequent editions or reprints.

This book is copyright ©2023 by Wisdom University with all rights reserved. It is illegal to redistribute, copy, or create derivative works from this book whole or in parts. No parts of this report may be reproduced or retransmitted in any forms whatsoever without the written expressed and signed permission from the publisher.

Printed in Great Britain
by Amazon